Learning to play a musical instrument is one of the most satisfying experiences a person can have. Being able to play along with other musicians makes that even more rewarding. This collection of sing-along songs is designed to make it easy to enjoy the fun of gathering with friends and family to make music together.

The music for each song displays the chord diagrams for five instruments: ukulele, baritone ukulele, guitar, mandolin and banjo. The chord diagrams indicate basic, commonly used finger positions. More advanced players can substitute alternate chord formations.

Arranged by Mark Phillips

ISBN 978-1-70517-603-0

Visit Hal Leonard Online at
www.halleonard.com

World headquarters, contact:
Hal Leonard
7777 West Bluemound Road
Milwaukee, WI 53213
Email: info@halleonard.com

In Europe, contact:
Hal Leonard Europe Limited
1 Red Place
London, W1K 6PL
Email: info@halleonardeurope.com

In Australia, contact:
Hal Leonard Australia Pty. Ltd.
4 Lentara Court
Cheltenham, Victoria, 3192 Australia
Email: info@halleonard.com.au

Standard Ukulele

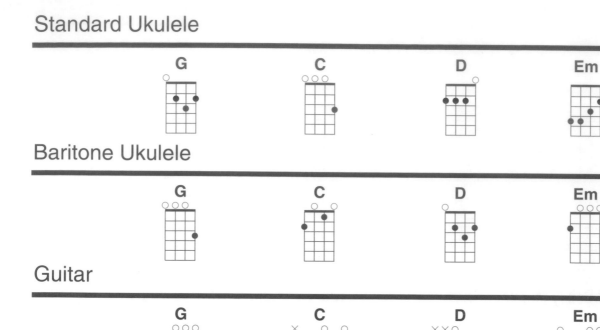

Baritone Ukulele

Guitar

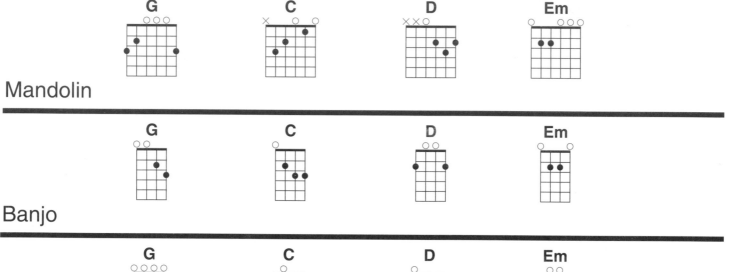

Mandolin

Banjo

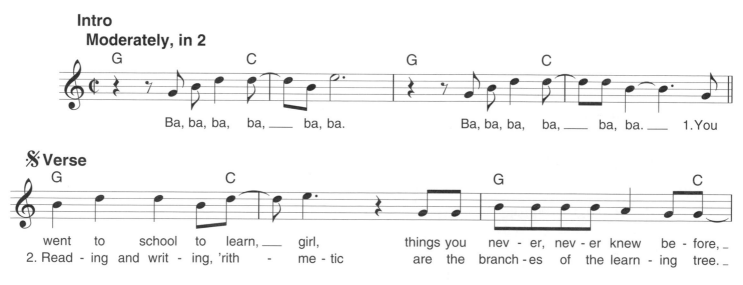

ABC

Words and Music by Alphonso Mizell, Frederick Perren, Deke Richards and Berry Gordy

Intro
Moderately, in 2

Ba, ba, ba, ba, ___ ba, ba.   Ba, ba, ba, ba, ___ ba, ba. ___ 1. You

Verse

went to school to learn, ___ girl,   things you nev-er, nev-er knew be-fore, _
2. Read-ing and writ-ing, 'rith - me-tic   are the branch-es of the learn-ing tree. _

Standard Ukulele

Baritone Ukulele

Guitar

Mandolin

Banjo

All Along the Watchtower
Words and Music by Bob Dylan

Verse
Moderately fast

1. "There must be some way out of here,"
2., 3. *See additional lyrics*

said the jok - er to the thief. ___ "There's too much __ con - fu -

- sion, I can't get ___ no re - lief. ___

Bus' - ness - men, _ they drink my wine, _ plow - men _ dig my earth. _

___ None of them a - long ___ the line ___

know what an - y of it is worth." ___

Play 3 times

Additional Lyrics

2. "No reason to get excited," the thief, he kindly spoke.
   "There are many here among us who feel that life is but a joke.
   But you and I, we've been through that, and this not our fate.
   So let us not talk falsely now, the hour's getting late."

3. All along the watchtower, princes kept the view,
   While all the women came and went, barefoot servants, too.
   Outside in the distance a wildcat did growl.
   Two riders were approaching, the wind began to howl.

Standard Ukulele

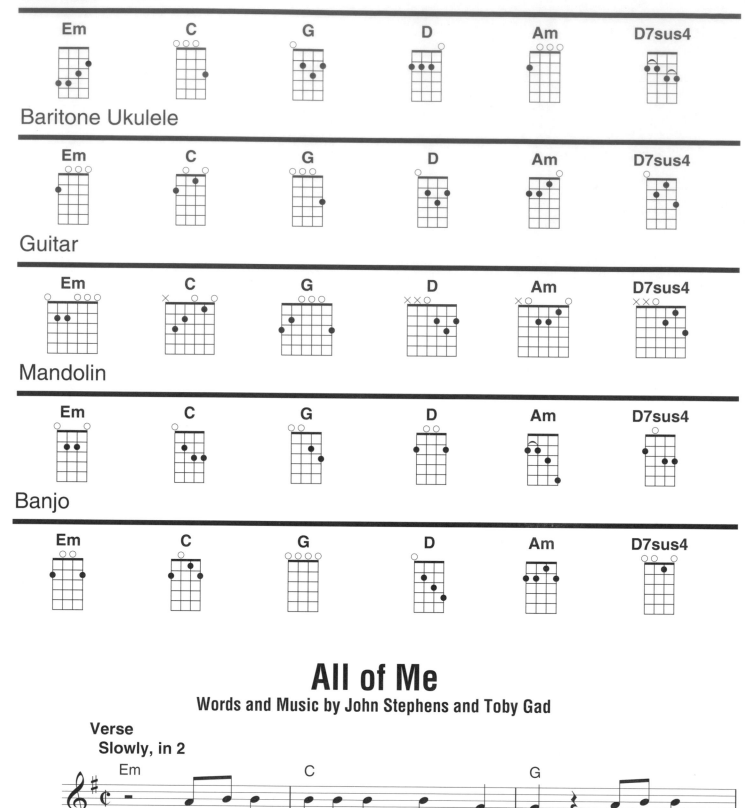

Baritone Ukulele

Guitar

Mandolin

Banjo

All of Me
Words and Music by John Stephens and Toby Gad

Verse
Slowly, in 2

1. What would I do with-out your smart mouth draw-in' me
2. How man-y times do I have to tell you, e - ven when you're

in and you kick-ing me out? ___ You've got my head spin-nin', no kid-din'; I
cry - ing you're beau-ti-ful too? ___ The world is beat - ing you down; I'm ___ a-

Baby Shark

Traditional Nursery Rhyme
Arranged by Pinkfong and KidzCastle

Standard Ukulele

E   B7   A

Baritone Ukulele

E   B7   A

Guitar

E   B7   A

Mandolin

E   B7 4fr   A

Banjo

E   B7   A

Bad Moon Rising

Words and Music by John Fogerty

Verse
Moderately, in 2

E   B7   A   E

1. I see   a   bad ___ moon a - ris - ing.
2. I hear   hur - ri - canes a - blow - ing.
3. Hope you   got your things to - geth - er.

B7   A

I see   trou - ble on   the way. ___
I know   the end   is   com - ing soon. ___
Hope you   are quite pre - pared   to   die. ___

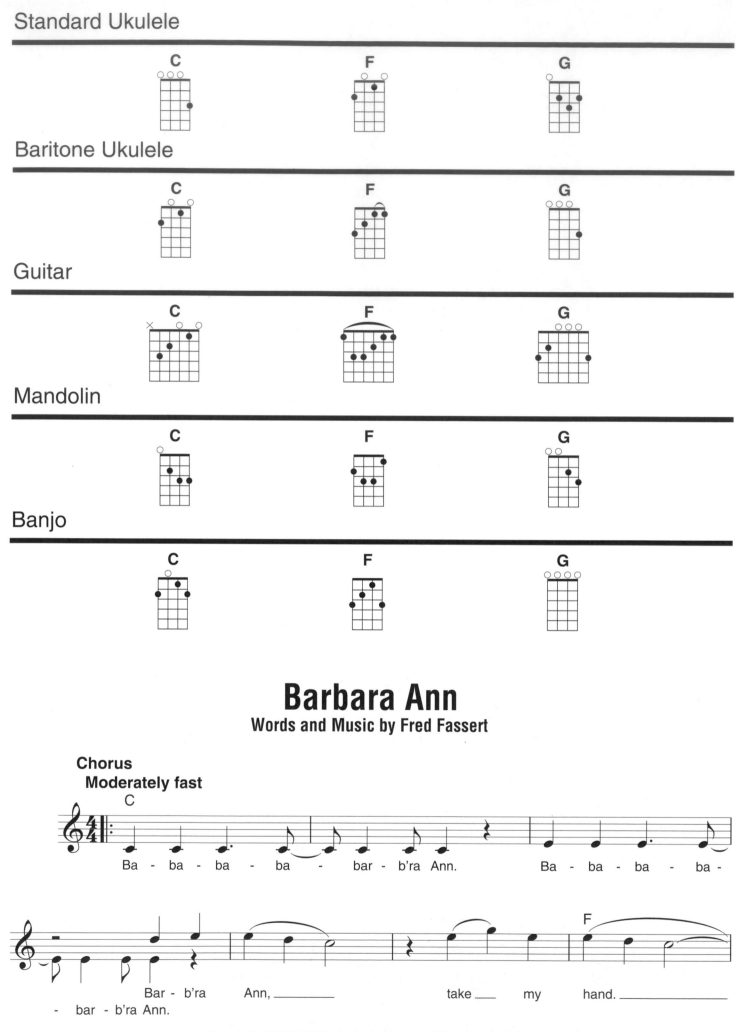

Barbara Ann
Words and Music by Fred Fassert

Standard Ukulele

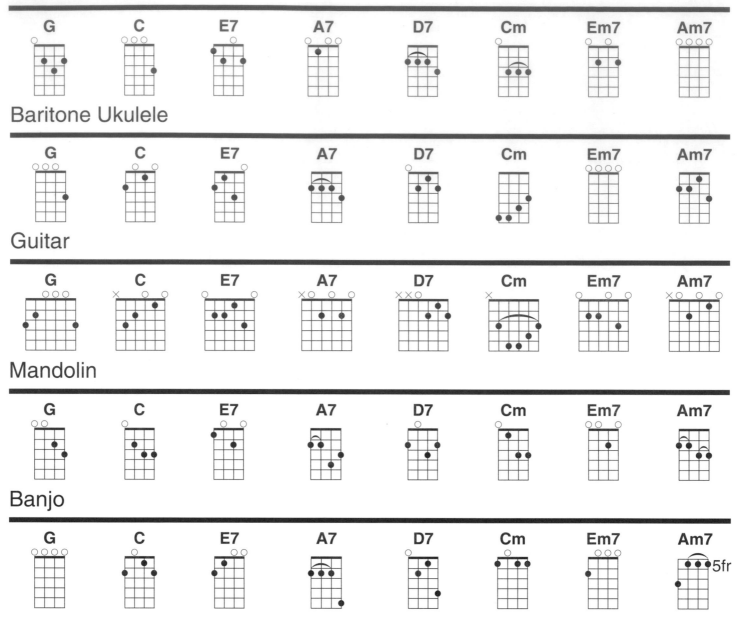

Baritone Ukulele

Guitar

Mandolin

Banjo

The Bare Necessities
from THE JUNGLE BOOK
Words and Music by Terry Gilkyson

Standard Ukulele

Am   D   G   G#°7   Em   Bm   C   Gmaj7

Baritone Ukulele

Am   D   G   G#°7   Em   Bm   C   Gmaj7

Guitar

Am   D   G   G#°7   Em   Bm   C   Gmaj7

Mandolin

Am   D   G   G#°7   Em   Bm   C   Gmaj7

Banjo

Am   D   G   G#°7   Em   Bm   C   Gmaj7

Bennie and the Jets
Words and Music by Elton John and Bernie Taupin

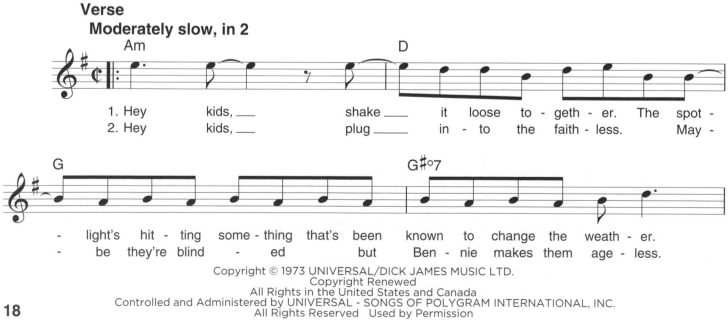

Verse
Moderately slow, in 2

1. Hey kids, ___ shake ___ it loose to - geth - er. The spot -
2. Hey kids, ___ plug ___ in - to the faith - less. May -

- light's hit - ting some - thing that's been known to change the weath - er.
- be they're blind - ed but Ben - nie makes them age - less.

Am .... **D**

We'll kill the fat-ted calf ____ to-night so ____ stick a-round. ____
We shall ____ sur-vive; ____ let us take our-selves a - long. ____

Em .... **Am**

_____ You're gon-na hear e-lec - tric mu -
_____ Where we fight ____ our par-ents out in the streets ____

Bm .... **C**

- sic, sol - id walls of sound. ____ Say,
____ to find who's right and who's wrong. ____ Oh,

Chorus

Gmaj7 .... **Am**

Can-dy and Ron - nie, have you seen them yet? Oh, ____ but they're so ____ spaced out, ____

.... **C**

____ Be - Be - Be - Be - Be - Ben-nie and the Jets. Oh, ____

Gmaj7 .... **Am**

____ but they're weird ____ and they're won - der - ful. Oh Ben - nie, she's ____ real - ly keen. ____

.... **C** .... **D**

She's got e - lec - tric boots, a mo - hair suit. You know I

Em .... **G** .... **C**

read it in a mag - a - zine. _____ Oh, _____

.... **D** **Gmaj7**

Be - Be - Be - Ben - nie and the Jets.

19

Standard Ukulele

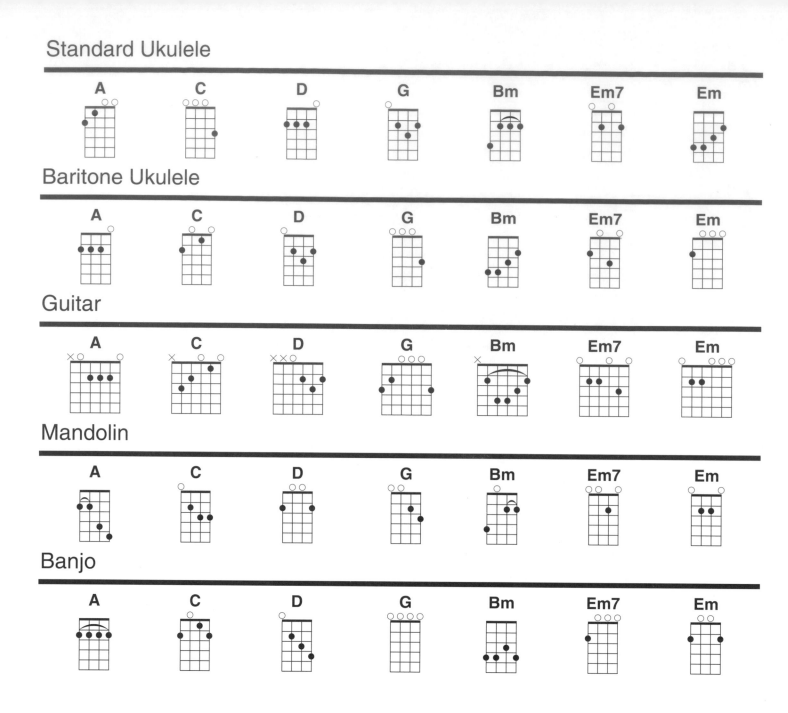

Baritone Ukulele

Guitar

Mandolin

Banjo

Cat's in the Cradle
Words and Music by Harry Chapin and Sandy Chapin

%. Verse

Moderately slow, in 2

1. My child ar-rived __ just the oth-er day; he came to the world in the
2., 3., 4. *See additional lyrics*

u - su - al way. __ But there were planes to catch ___ and bills to pay. __

He learned to walk while I was a-way. And he was talk-in' 'fore I knew it, and as he grew he'd say, "I'm gon-na be like you, Dad. You know I'm gon-na be like you." And the cat's in the cra-dle and the sil-ver spoon, __ lit-tle boy blue and the man __ in the moon. __

1., 2. "When you com-in' home, Dad?" "I don't know when,
3., 4. "When you com-in' home, Son?" "I don't know when,
but we'll get to-geth-er then. __

(1., 2., 3. You know we'll)
(4. We're gon-na) have a good time then."

2. My
3. Well, he

4. I've

Coda

And as I hung up the phone, it oc-curred to me, __ he'd grown up just like me. My boy was just like me. And the

To Coda

%. Chorus

Fine 1., 2.   3. *D.S. al Coda*

D.S.S. al Fine

Additional Lyrics

2. My son turned ten just the other day.
   He said, "Thanks for the ball, Dad; come on let's play.
   Can you teach me to throw?" I said, "Not today;
   I got a lot to do." He said, "That's okay."
   And he, he walked away, but his smile never dimmed.
   It said, I'm gonna be like him, yeah.
   You know I'm gonna be like him.

3. Well, he came from college just the other day,
   So much like a man I just had to say,
   "Son, I'm proud of you, can you sit for a while?"
   He shook his head and then said with a smile,
   "What I'd really like, Dad, is to borrow the car keys.
   See you later. Can I have them please?"

4. I've long since retired, my son's moved away.
   I called him up just the other day.
   I said, "I'd like to see you if you don't mind."
   He said, "I'd love to, Dad, if I can find the time.
   You see, my new job's a hassle and the kids have the flu.
   But it's sure nice talking to you, Dad.
   It's been sure nice talking to you."

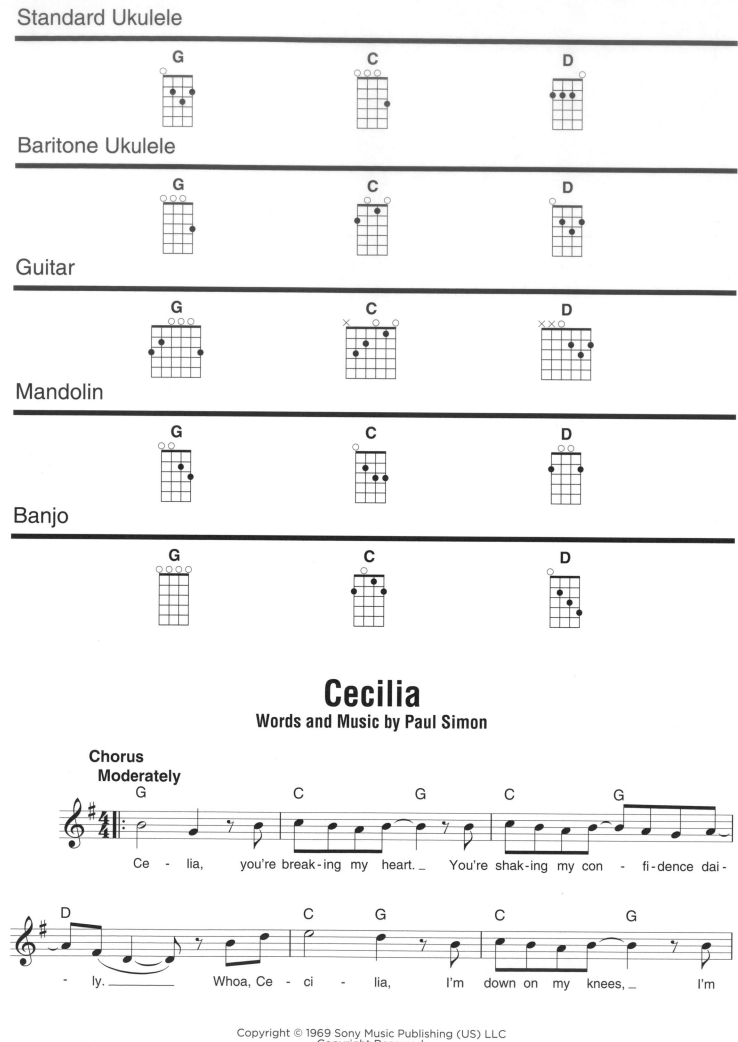

Cecilia

Words and Music by Paul Simon

Come on Get Higher

Words and Music by Matt Nathanson and Mark Weinberg

Verse
Moderately

1. I miss the sound of your _ voice, ___   and I miss the rush of your _ skin. _
2. I miss the sound of your _ voice, ___   the loud - est thing in my _ head. _

___ And I miss the still of the si - lence   as you _
___ And I ache _ to re - mem - ber   all the vi' -

25

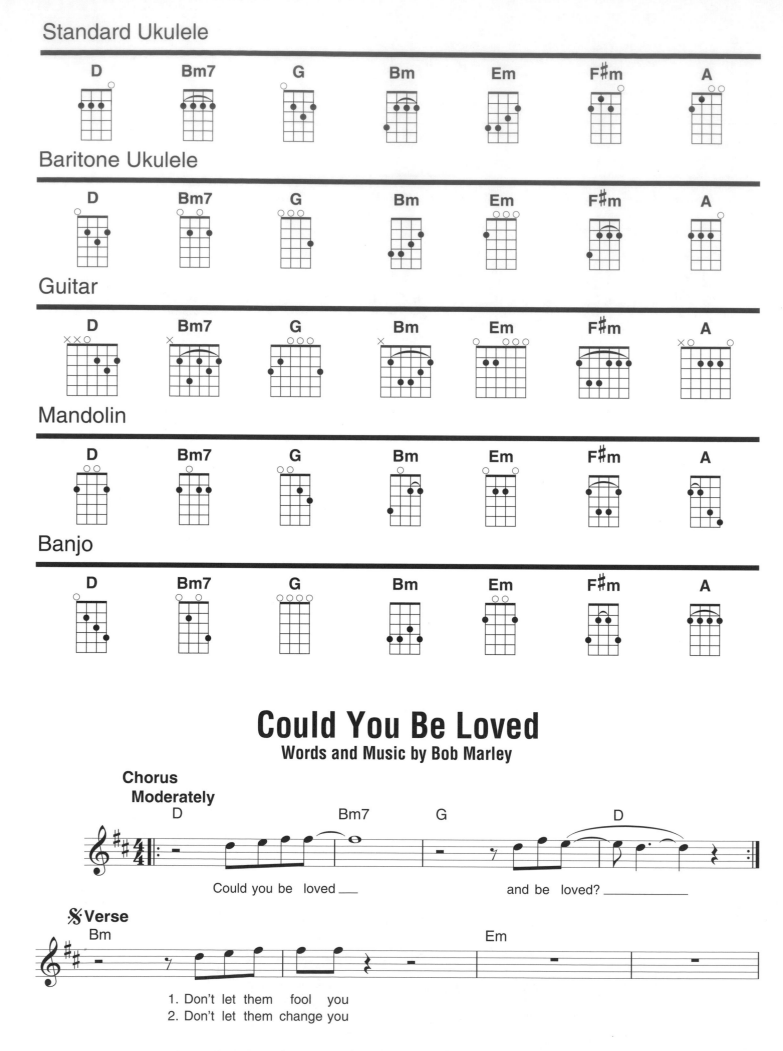

Could You Be Loved

Words and Music by Bob Marley

Could you be loved ___ and be loved? _____

1. Don't let them fool you
2. Don't let them change you

Standard Ukulele

Baritone Ukulele

Guitar

Mandolin

Banjo

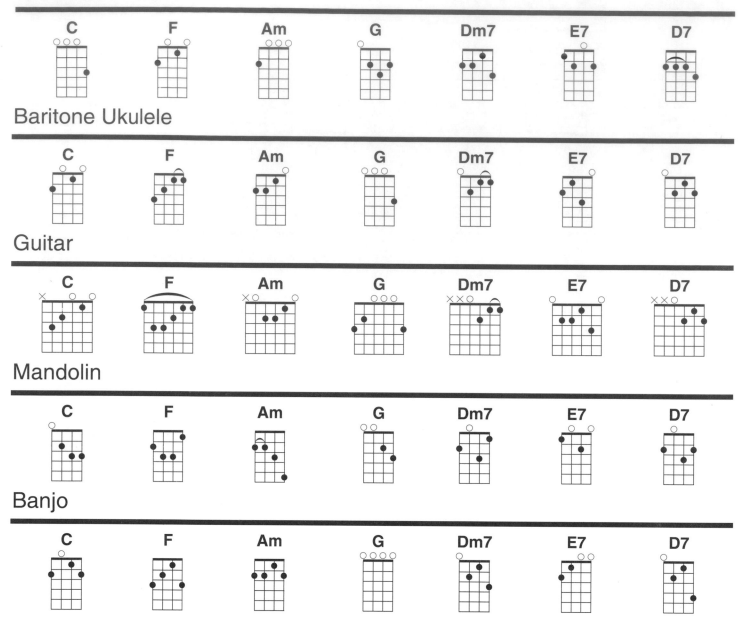

Dancing Queen
Words and Music by Benny Andersson, Bjorn Ulvaeus and Stig Anderson

Verse
Moderately, in 2

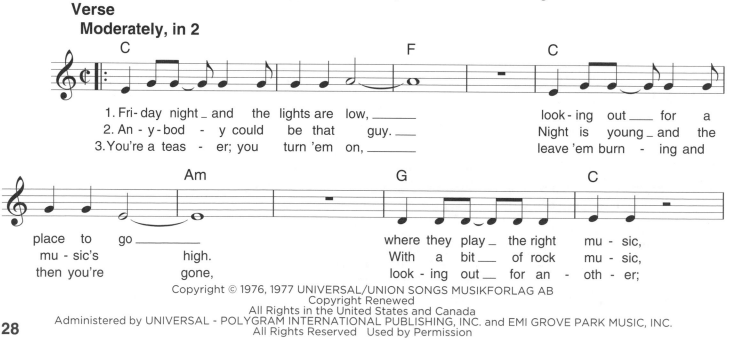

1. Fri-day night _ and the lights are low, _____ look-ing out ___ for a
2. An-y-bod-y could be that guy. _ Night is young _ and the
3. You're a teas-er; you turn 'em on, _____ leave 'em burn - ing and

place to go _____ where they play _ the right mu-sic,
mu-sic's high. With a bit __ of rock mu-sic,
then you're gone, look-ing out__ for an-oth-er;

Day-O
(The Banana Boat Song)
Words and Music by Irving Burgie and William Attaway

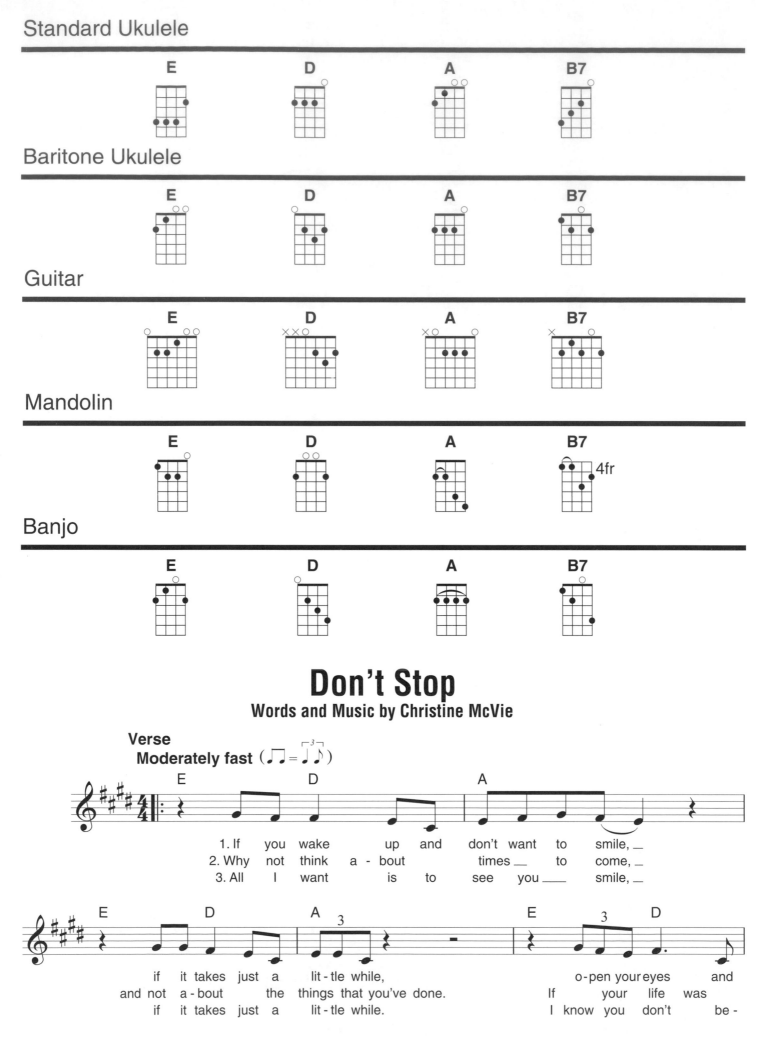

Standard Ukulele

Baritone Ukulele

Guitar

Mandolin

Banjo

Don't Stop
Words and Music by Christine McVie

Verse
Moderately fast

1. If you wake up and don't want to smile, __
2. Why not think a - bout times __ to come, __
3. All I want is to see you __ smile, __

if it takes just a lit - tle while,
and not a - bout the things that you've done.
if it takes just a lit - tle while.

o-pen your eyes and
If your life was
I know you don't be -

look at the day. ___ You'll see things in a dif-f'rent ___ way. _____
bad to you, just think what to-mor-row will do. _____
lieve that it's true. I nev-er meant an-y harm ___ to you. _____

Chorus

Don't stop think-ing a-bout to-mor - row. Don't stop;

it - 'll soon ___ be here. _____ It - 'll be _____

Play 3 times

bet-ter than be - fore. _ Yes ter-day's gone, ___ yes - ter-day's gone. _____

Chorus

Don't stop think-ing a-bout to-mor - row. Don't stop;

it - 'll soon ___ be here. _____ It - 'll be _____

bet-ter than be - fore. _ Yes-ter-day's gone, ___ yes - ter-day's gone. _____

Outro

Oo, _____ don't you look ___ back.

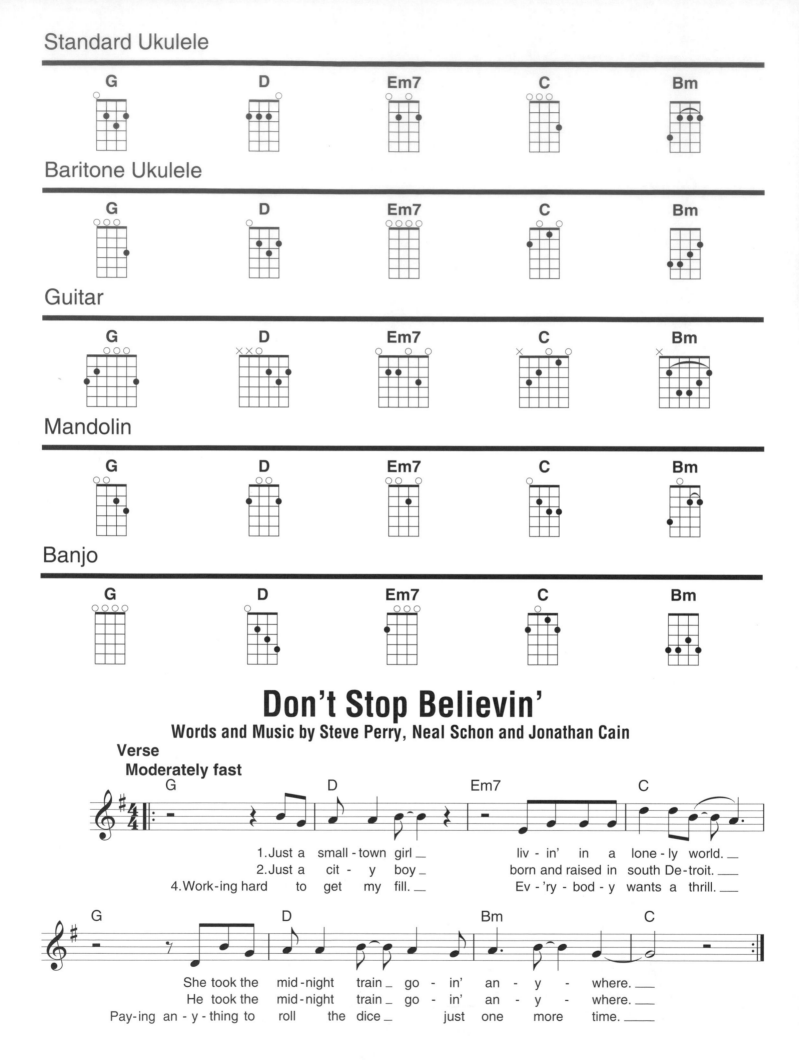

Standard Ukulele

Baritone Ukulele

Guitar

Mandolin

Banjo

Don't Stop Believin'

Words and Music by Steve Perry, Neal Schon and Jonathan Cain

Verse
Moderately fast

1. Just a small-town girl _ liv-in' in a lone-ly world. _
2. Just a cit-y boy _ born and raised in south De-troit. _
4. Work-ing hard to get my fill. _ Ev-'ry-bod-y wants a thrill. _

She took the mid-night train _ go-in' an-y-where. _
He took the mid-night train _ go-in' an-y-where. _
Pay-ing an-y-thing to roll the dice _ just one more time. _

Verse

3. A sing-er in a smok-y room, _ the smell of wine and cheap per-fume. _
5. Some will win, _ some will lose, _ some were born to sing the blues. _

For a smile _ they can share the night; _ it goes on and on _ and on _ and on. _
Oh, the mov-ie nev - er ends; _ it goes on and on _ and on _ and on. _

Chorus

Stran - gers _ wait - ing _ up and down the boul - e - vard, _ their

shad - ows _ search - ing _ in the night. _

Street - light _ peo - ple, _ liv - ing just to find e - mo - tion,

To Coda

hid - ing _ some - where _ in the night. _

D.C. al Coda (no repeat)

Coda

some - where in the night. _

Outro

Don't _ stop _ be-

liev - in'. _ Hold on to the feel - in'. _ Street - light _

peo - ple. _ Don't _ stop.

Standard Ukulele

Baritone Ukulele

Guitar

Mandolin

Banjo

Drift Away
Words and Music by Mentor Williams

Verse
Moderately slow, in 2

1. Day af - ter day, I'm ___ more con - fused, ___
2. Be - gin - nin' to think that I'm wast - in' time. ___
3. Thanks for the joy that you've giv - en me. ___

yet I look for the light through the pour - in' rain. ___
I don't un - der - stand the things ___ I do. ___
I wan't you to know ___ I be - lieve in your song. ___

You know that's a game that I hate to lose,
The world out-side looks so un-kind.
In rhy-thm and rhyme and har-mo-ny,

and I'm feel-in' the strain; ain't it a shame?
Now I'm count-ing on you to car-ry me through. } Oh,
you've helped me a-long, mak-in' me strong.

Chorus

give me the beat, boys, and free my soul. I wan-na get lost in your rock 'n' roll and

drift a-way. Oh, give me the beat, boys, and free my soul. I

wan-na get lost in your rock 'n' roll and drift a-way.

To Coda ⊕
G   D   C   D   G   D7sus4   G

Bridge

And when my mind is free, you know a mel-o-dy can

move me. And when I'm feel-in' blue,

D.C. al Coda   ⊕ **Coda**

the gui-tar's com-in' through to soothe me.

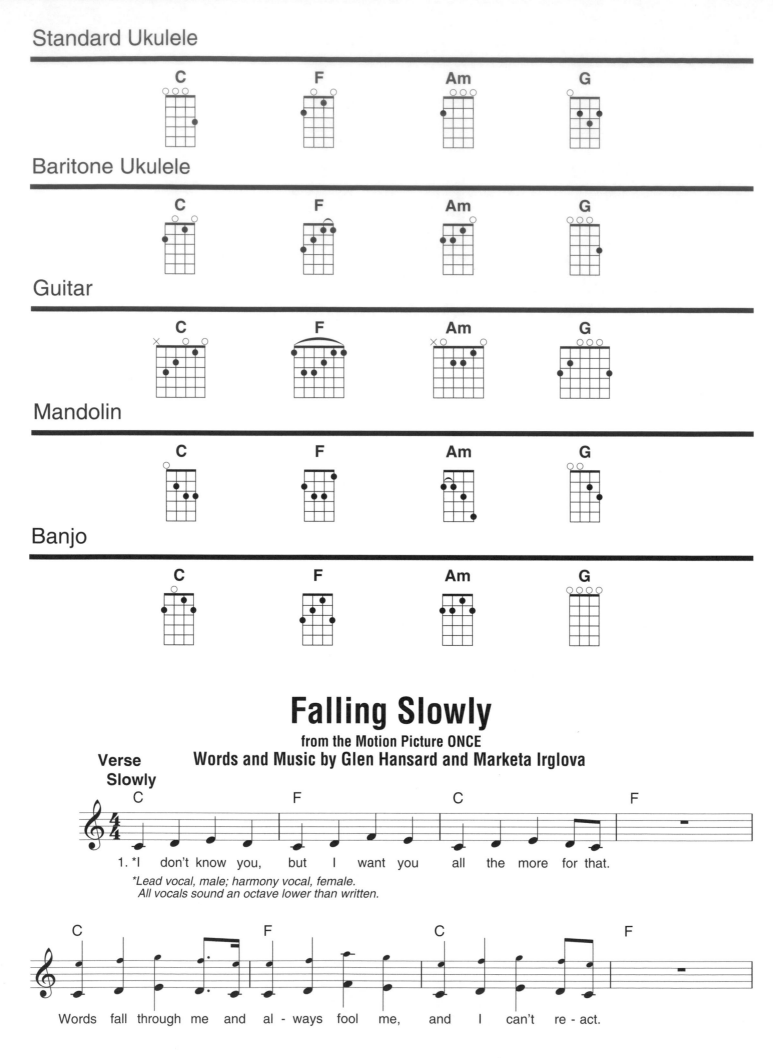

Standard Ukulele

C   F   Am   G

Baritone Ukulele

C   F   Am   G

Guitar

C   F   Am   G

Mandolin

C   F   Am   G

Banjo

C   F   Am   G

Falling Slowly

from the Motion Picture ONCE
Words and Music by Glen Hansard and Marketa Irglova

**Verse
Slowly**

C   F   C   F

1. *I don't know you, but I want you all the more for that.

*Lead vocal, male; harmony vocal, female.
All vocals sound an octave lower than written.

C   F   C   F

Words fall through me and al-ways fool me, and I can't re-act.

Standard Ukulele

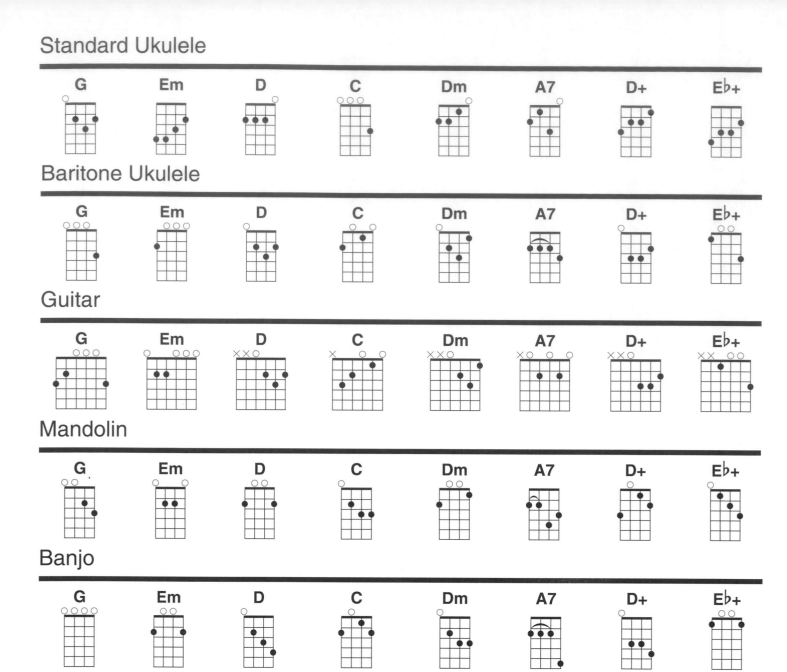

Baritone Ukulele

Guitar

Mandolin

Banjo

From Me to You
Words and Music by John Lennon and Paul McCartney

Intro
Moderately fast

Da, da, da, da, da, dum, dum, da. Da, da, da, da, da, dum, dum,

Verse

da.   1. If there's an - y - thing that you want, ___ if there's

ev - 'ry - thing that you want, ___ like a

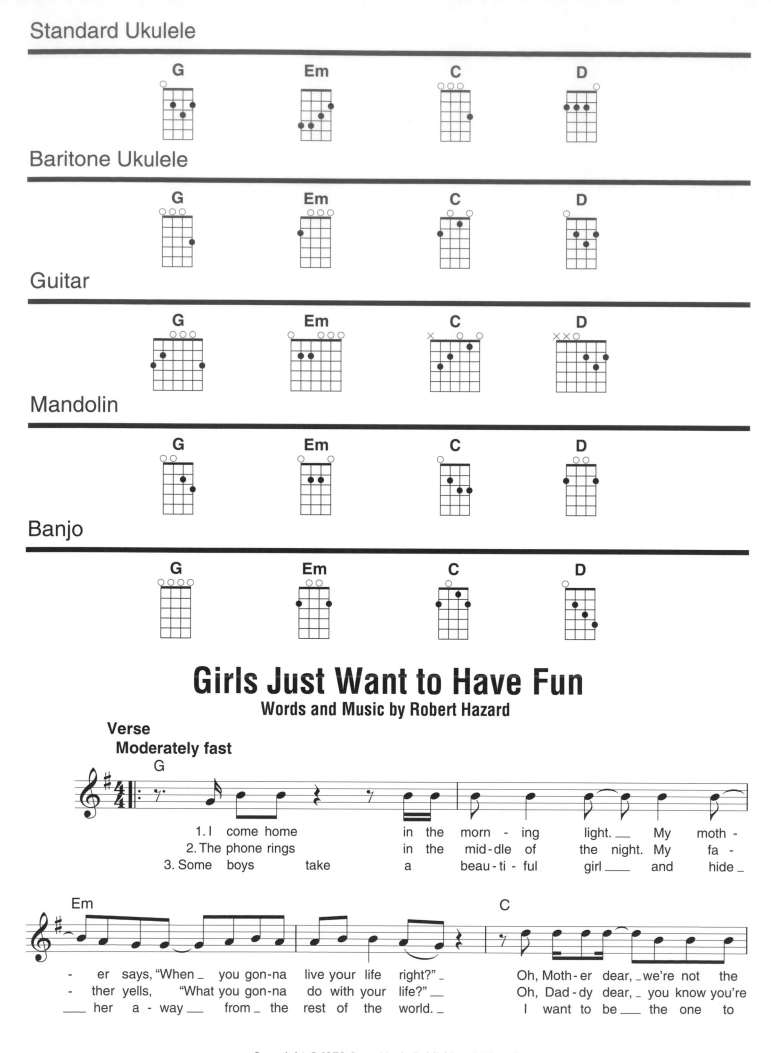

Girls Just Want to Have Fun

Words and Music by Robert Hazard

Verse
Moderately fast

1. I come home in the morn-ing light. ___ My moth-
2. The phone rings in the mid-dle of the night. My fa-
3. Some boys take a beau-ti-ful girl ___ and hide ___

- er says, "When ___ you gon-na live your life right?" ___ Oh, Moth-er dear, ___ we're not the
- ther yells, "What you gon-na do with your life?" ___ Oh, Dad-dy dear, ___ you know you're
- ___ her a-way ___ from ___ the rest of the world. ___ I want to be ___ the one to

Standard Ukulele

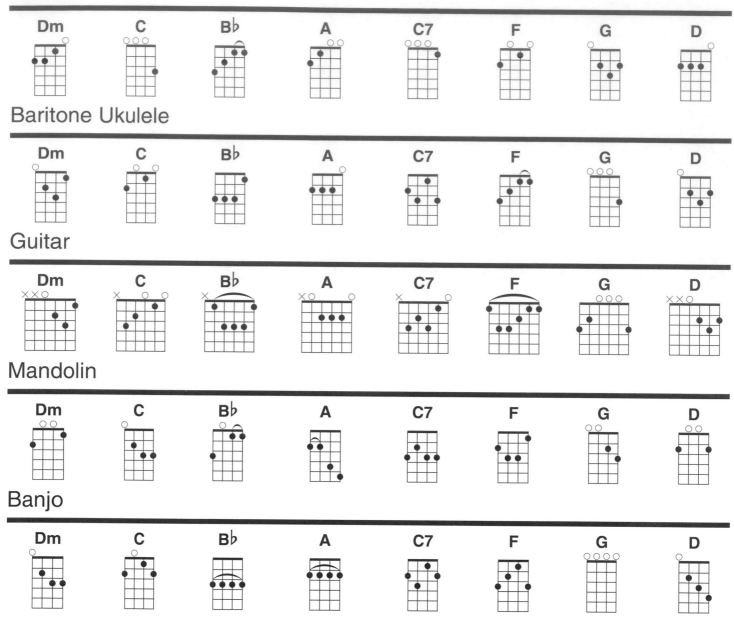

Baritone Ukulele

Guitar

Mandolin

Banjo

Good Vibrations
Words and Music by Brian Wilson and Mike Love

Verse
Moderately fast

1. I, _____ I love the col-or-ful clothes she wears _____
2. Close my eyes, she's some-how clos-er now. _____

and the way the sun-light plays up-on ___ her hair. _____
Soft-ly smile, I know she must _ be kind. _

I _____ hear the sound of a
Then _____ I look

gen - tle word _____ on the wind that lifts her
in her eyes. _____ She goes with me to a

per - fume through the air. _____
blos - som world. _

Chorus

I'm pick - ing up good vi - bra - tions. She's gi - ving me

ex - ci - ta - tions. I'm pick - ing up good vi - bra - tions.

She's gi - ving me ex - ci - ta - tions. Good, good, good, good _ vi - bra -

- tions. _____ Good, good, good, good _ vi - bra -

Outro

- tions. _____ Na, na, na, na, na, na, na, na.

Na, na, na, na, na, na, na, na. Na, na, na, na, na,

na, na, na. Na, na, na, na, na, na, na, na.

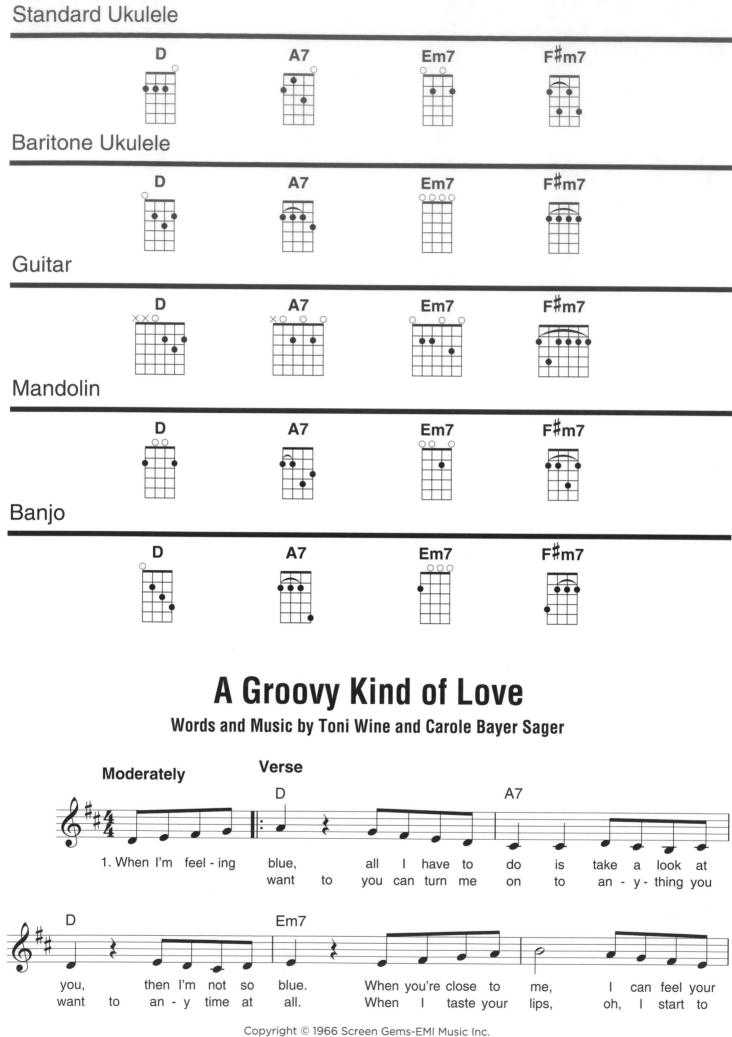

A Groovy Kind of Love

Words and Music by Toni Wine and Carole Bayer Sager

Standard Ukulele

Baritone Ukulele

Guitar

Mandolin

Banjo

Happy

from DESPICABLE ME 2
Words and Music by Pharrell Williams

Verse
Moderately fast

E7 N.C.   E7   G   A   B

1. It might seem cra - zy what I'm 'bout to say: _____
2. Here come bad news, _____ talk - in' this and that. _____

A   E7   N.C.

Sun - shine, _ she's here; _____ you can take a break.
Well, gim - me all you got, _____ no _____ hold - ing back. _____

I'm a hot air bal - loon ___
Well, I should prob - 'bly warn ___

___ that could go to space ___
___ you, I'll be just ___ fine. ___

with the air ___

___ like I don't care, ___ ba - by, by the way. ___
No of-fense to you, ___ don't ___ waste your time. ___

Here's why:

Chorus

Huh! (Be-cause I'm Hap - py.) Clap a - long if ___ you feel ___ like a

room with - out a roof. ___ (Be-cause I'm Hap - py.) Clap a - long if ___

___ you feel ___ like hap - pi - ness is the truth. ___ (Be-cause I'm

Hap - py.) Clap a - long ___ if ___ you know ___ what hap - pi - ness is to you. ___

(Be-cause I'm Hap - py.) Clap a - long if ___ you feel ___ like

1. that's what you wan - na do. ___

2. ___ *Come on.*

Hey, Soul Sister

Words and Music by Pat Monahan, Espen Lind and Amund Bjorklund

I know I would-n't for-get ya, and so I went and let you blow _ my mind. _
You gave my life di - rec-tion, a game show love con - nec-tion we can't de -

___ ny.
Your sweet moon-beam, the smell of you in ev - 'ry
I'm so ob - sessed; my heart is bound to beat right

sin - gle dream I dream. _ I knew when we col - lid - ed you're the one I have de -
out my un -trimmed chest. _ I be-lieve in you; like a vir - gin, you're Ma -

cid - ed who's one of my kind. ___
don - na, and I'm al - ways gon - na wan - na blow _ your mind.

Chorus

Hey, soul sis - ter, ain't ___ that Mis - ter Mis -ter on the ra - di - o, ster - e - o? The

way you move ain't fair, you know. Hey, soul sis - ter, I ___ don't wan -na miss a sin - gle

thing you do _____ to - night. Hey, ___ hey, ___

1. ___ hey. ___
2. To - night.

51

Standard Ukulele

Baritone Ukulele

Guitar

Mandolin

Banjo

Ho Hey

Words and Music by Jeremy Fraites and Wesley Schultz

Verse
Moderately slow, in 2

1.(Ho!) I've been tryin' to do ____ it right. (Hey!) I've been liv-in' a lone-

- ly life. ____ (Ho!) I've been sleep-in' here ____ in-stead. (Hey!) I've been sleep-in' in _

____ my bed, ____ (Ho!) I've been sleep-in' in ____ my bed. (Hey!)

53

Standard Ukulele

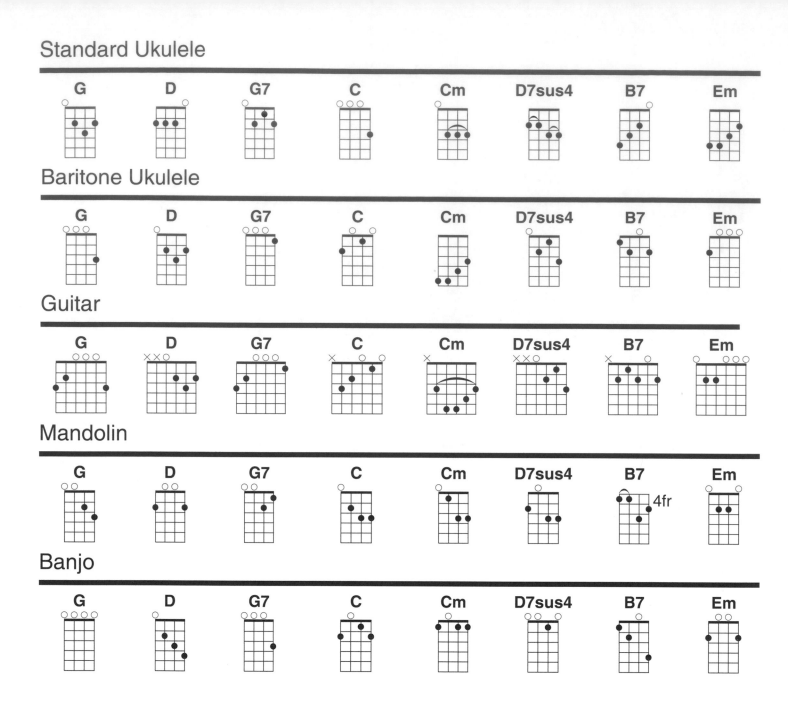

Baritone Ukulele

Guitar

Mandolin

Banjo

Hooked on a Feeling
Words and Music by Mark James

Verse
Moderately fast

1. I can't stop _ this feel - ing _____ deep in - side _ of me. _

Girl, you just _ don't re - al - ize _____ what you do _____ to me. _____

Pre-Chorus

When you hold ___ me in your arms ___ so tight, _ you let me ___ know ev-'ry-thing's _

Chorus

___ all right. _ I, _____ I'm hooked on a feel - ing, _____

___ high _ on be - liev - ing _____ that you're _ in love ___ with me. ___

To Coda

2. Your lips are sweet _ as can - dy; ___ the

taste stays on ___ my mind. ___ You just keep _ me thirst - y for ___ an -

oth - er cup _ of wine. ___ I've got it bad _ for you, ___ girl, ___ but

I don't need _ a cure. ___ I'll just stay _ ad - dict - ed and hope I can _

Pre-Chorus

___ en - dure _____ all the good ___ love when we're all ___ a - lone. _ Keep it up,

D.S. al Coda

Coda

___ girl; yeah, you turn ___ me on. ___

Standard Ukulele

Baritone Ukulele

Guitar

Mandolin

Banjo

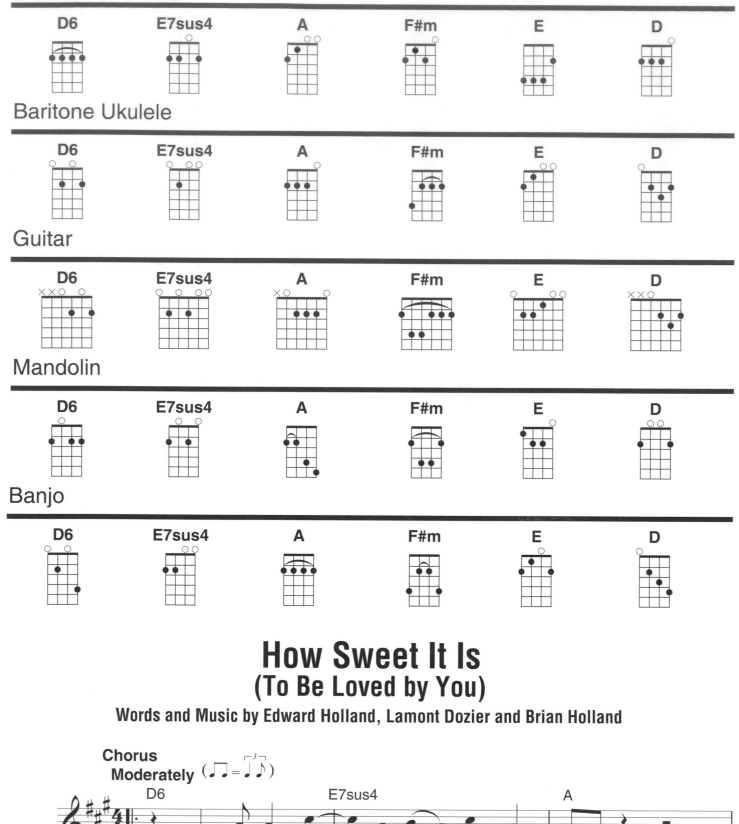

How Sweet It Is
(To Be Loved by You)

Words and Music by Edward Holland, Lamont Dozier and Brian Holland

How sweet it is ___ to be ___ loved by you. ___

How sweet it is ___ to be ___ loved by

2. Close my eyes at night
   And wonder what would I be without you in my life.
   Everything was just a bore;
   All the things I did, seems I've done 'em before.
   But you brightened up all my days
   With a love so sweet in so many ways.
   I want to stop and thank you, baby.
   I want to stop and thank you, baby.

3. You were better to me than I've been to myself.
   For me there's you and nobody else
   I want to stop and thank you, baby.
   I want to stop and thank you, baby.

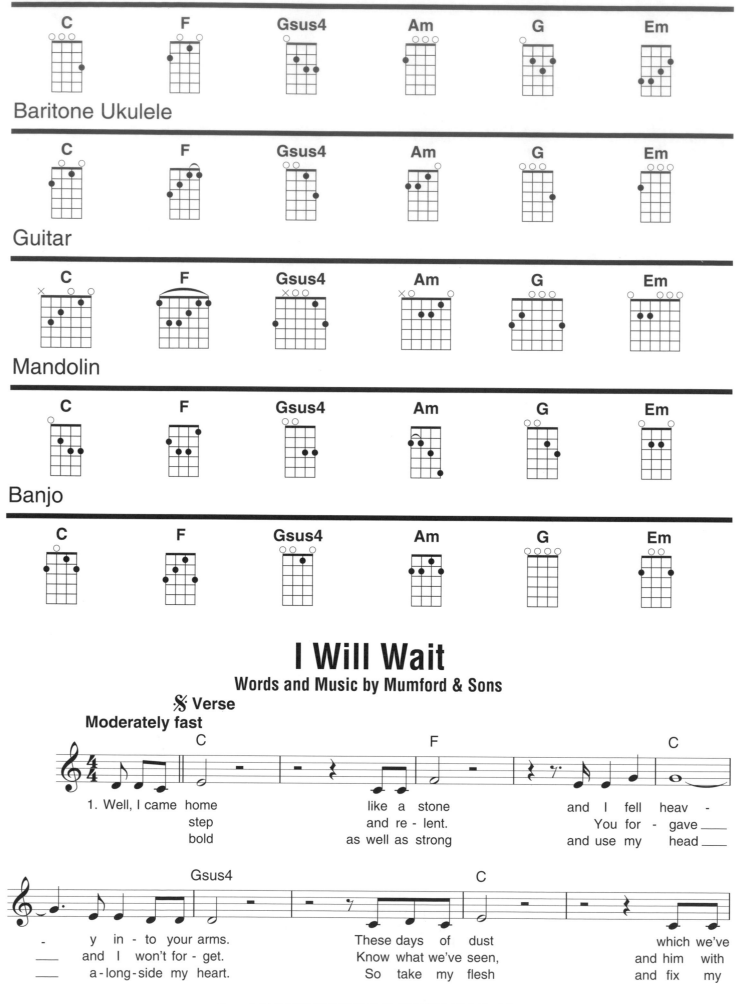

Standard Ukulele

Baritone Ukulele

Guitar

Mandolin

Banjo

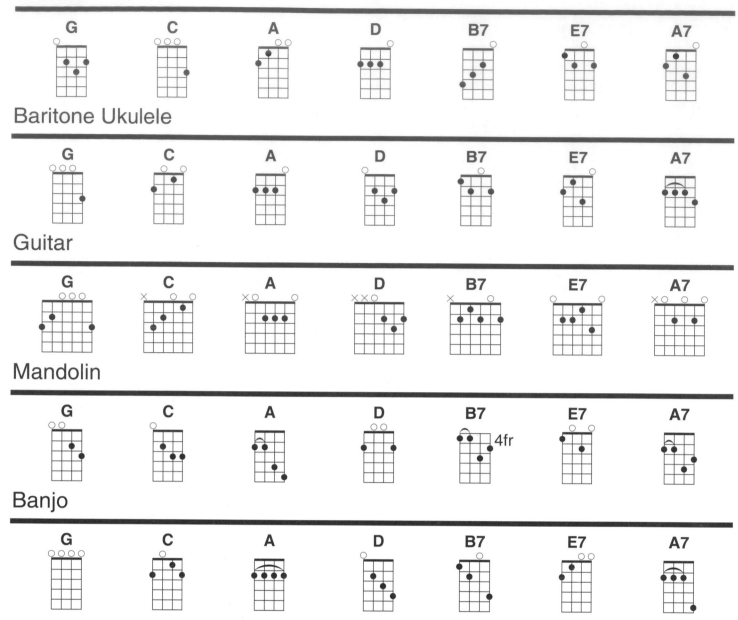

I'm Henry VIII, I Am

Words and Music by Fred Murray and R.P. Weston

Verse
Fast

G   C

1., 2. I'm Hen - er - y the Eighth, I am. Hen - er - y the Eighth, I

G

am, I am. ___ I got mar - ried to the wid - ow next door.

Iko Iko
Words and Music by Barbara Ann Hawkins, Joan Marie Johnson and Rosa Lee Hawkins

1. My grand-ma and your _ grand-ma _ sit-ting by the fi - re.
3. My flag boy and your _ flag boy _ sit-ting by the fi - re.

My grand-ma says to your grand-ma, _ } "I'm gon-na set your flag on fi - re." Talk - in' 'bout
My flag boy says to your flag boy, _ }

Standard Ukulele

Baritone Ukulele

Guitar

Mandolin

Banjo

Jessie's Girl
Words and Music by Rick Springfield

Verse
Moderately fast

D   A   Bm G   A D   A   Bm   G

1. Jes - sie is a friend; yeah, I know ___ he's been a good friend of mine. ___
long with the cha - rade; there does-n't seem to be a rea - son to change. ___

A D   A   Bm G   A   D

___ But late - ly some - thing's changed; ___ It ain't hard ___ to de - fine. Jes-sie's got
You know, I feel so dirt - y when they start ___ talk-in' cute. I wan-na tell

65

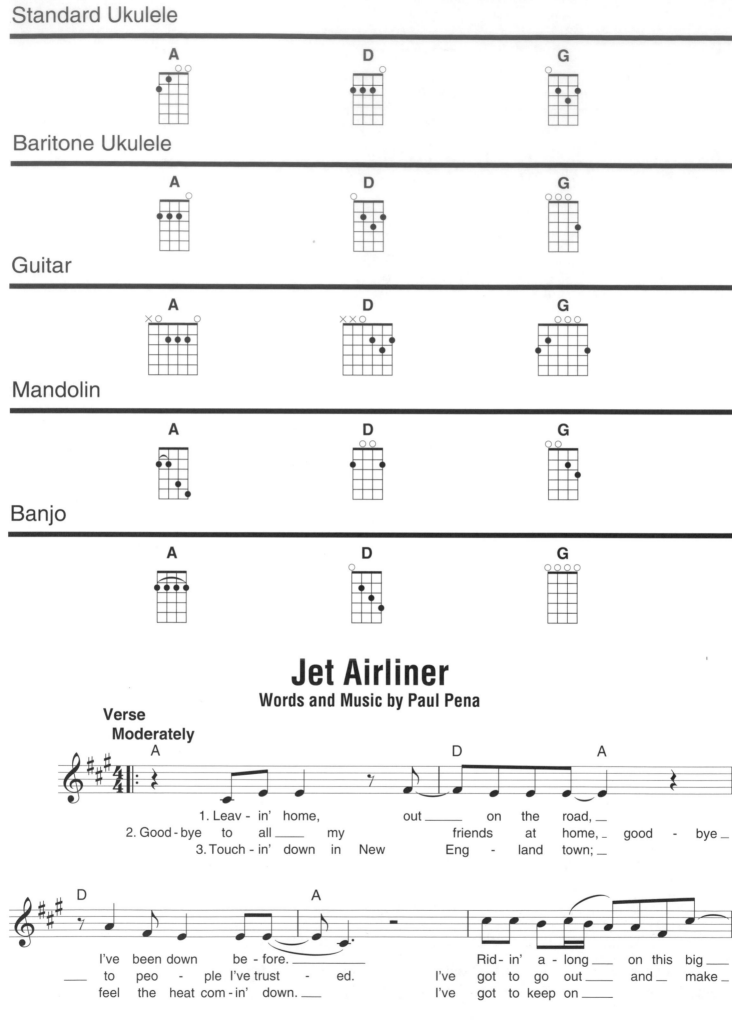

Jet Airliner

Words and Music by Paul Pena

Verse
Moderately

1. Leav - in' home, out ____ on the road, ____
2. Good - bye to all ____ my friends at home, _ good - bye _
3. Touch - in' down in New Eng - land town; _

I've been down be - fore. _____ Rid - in' a - long ____ on this big ____
____ to peo - ple I've trust - ed. I've got to go out ____ and make _
feel the heat com - in' down. ____ I've got to keep on ____

— ol' jet plane, ___ I've been think - in' a - bout ___ my ___ home. ___
— my ___ way. I might get rich, you know, I might get ___ bust -
keep - in' ___ on. ___ You know, the big wheel ___ keeps on

_____ But my love ___ light seems ___ so far ___
- ed. But my heart keeps call - in' me back -
spin - nin' a - round. And I'm go - in' with some ___ hes - i - ta -

___ a - way, ___ and I ___ feel like it's all ___ been done. ___
- wards ___ as I ___ get on the sev - en - o - sev - en.
- tion. ___ You know that I can sure - ly see that I

Some - bod - y's try'n' ___ to make ___ me stay. ___ You know, I've
Rid - in' high, ___ I got tears in my eyes. ___ You know, you
don't want ___ to get ___ caught up ___ in an - y of that

got to be mov - in' on. Oh. ___
got to go through hell be - fore you get to heav - en.
funk - y shit go - in' down ___ in the cit - y.

𝄋 Chorus

Big old jet ___ air - lin - er, ___ don't ___ car - ry me too far a - way. ___

___ Oh. ___ Big old jet ___ air - lin - er, ___ 'cause it's here ___

To Coda ⊕ | 1., 2. | 3. *D.S. al Coda* ⊕ **Coda**

___ that I've got to ___ stay. ___ ___ Oh. ___ ___

67

Standard Ukulele

Baritone Ukulele

Guitar

Mandolin

Banjo

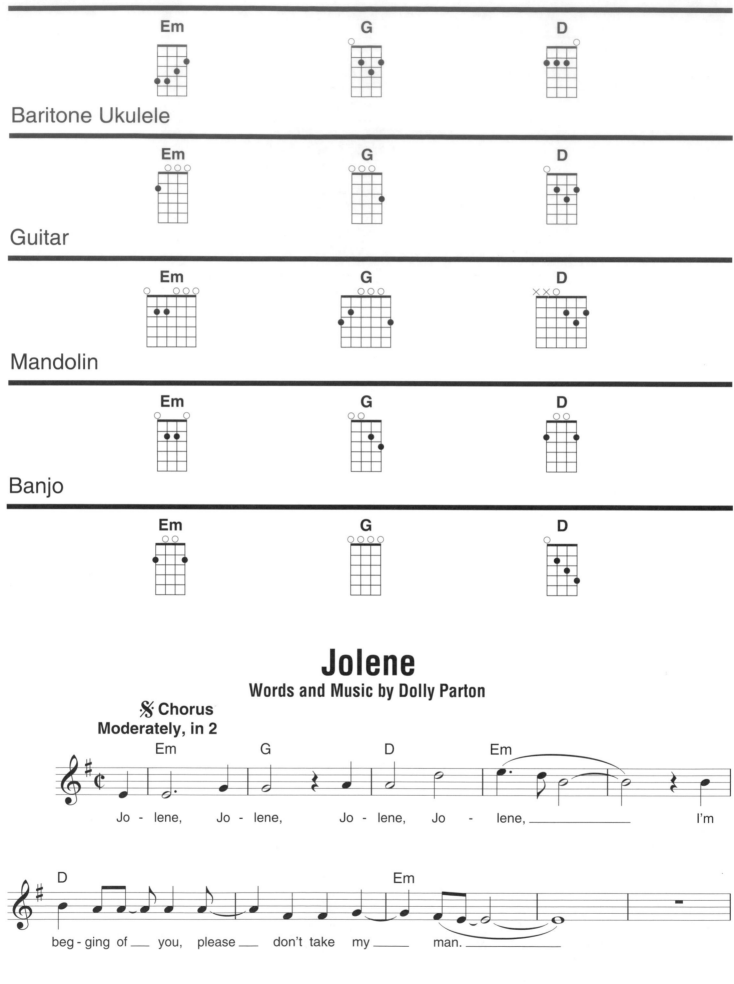

Jolene
Words and Music by Dolly Parton

Chorus
Moderately, in 2

Em   G   D   Em

Jo - lene, Jo - lene, Jo - lene, Jo - lene, _____ I'm

D   Em

beg - ging of __ you, please __ don't take my __ man.

Standard Ukulele

Baritone Ukulele

Guitar

Mandolin

Banjo

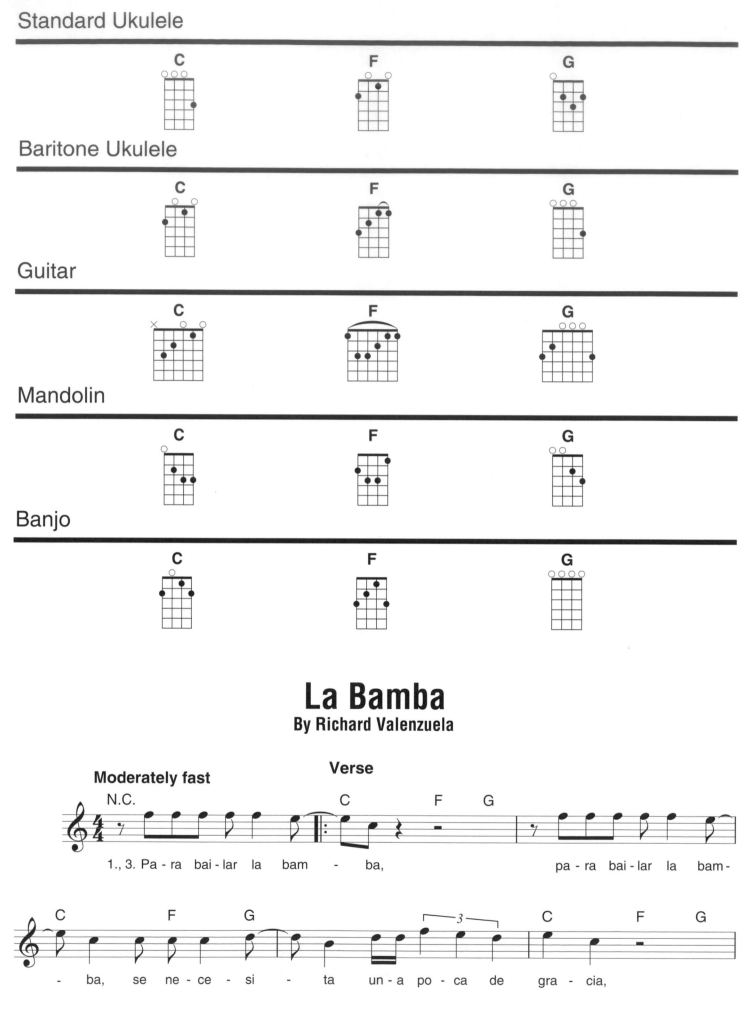

La Bamba

By Richard Valenzuela

un - a po - ca de gra - cia, pa_ra mi pa_ra ti, ___ y ar - ri - ba, ar - ri -

- ba; ar - ri - ba, ar - ri - ba, por ti se - ré, __

___ por ti se - ré, por ti se - ré. 2., 4. Yo no soy mar - i -

Verse

ne - ro. Yo no soy mar - i - ne - ro, soy cap - i - tan; _

___ soy cap - i - tan, ___ soy cap - i - tan. ___

Chorus

Bam - ba bam - ba. Bam - ba bam -

- ba. Bam - ba bam - ba,

ba... ___ 3. Pa - ra bai - lar la bam -

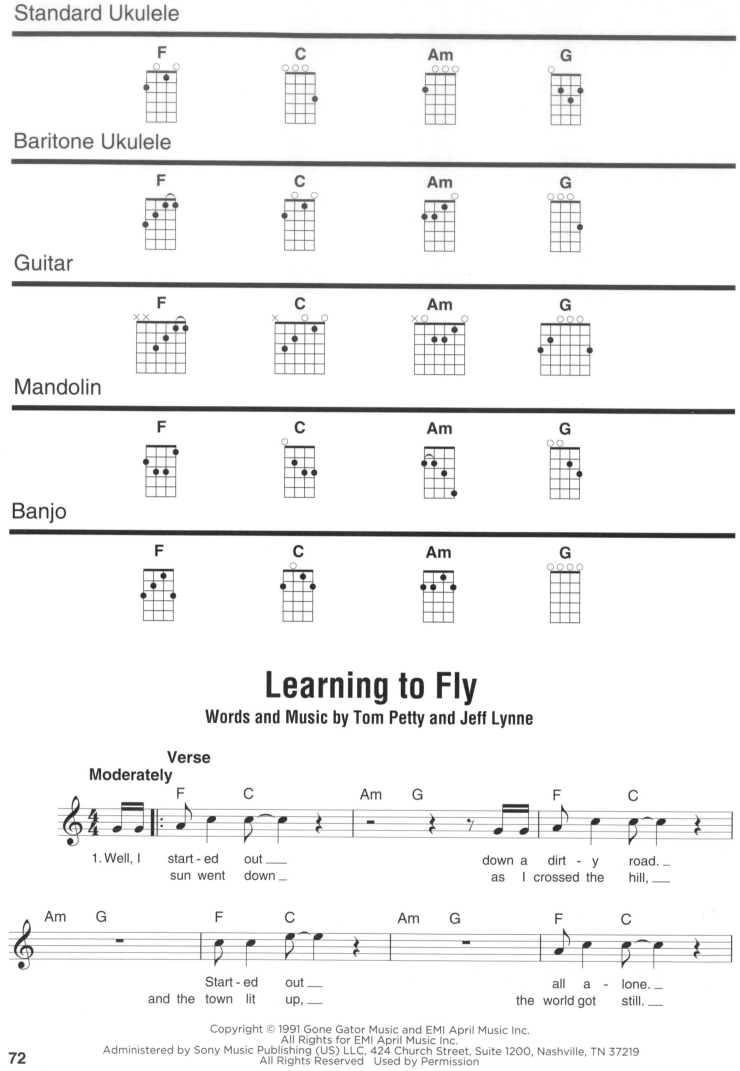

Learning to Fly

Words and Music by Tom Petty and Jeff Lynne

Standard Ukulele

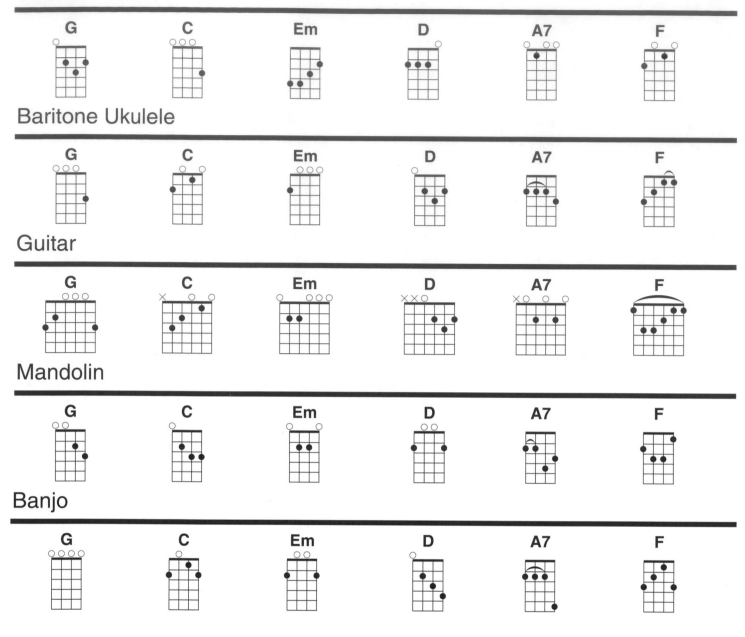

Baritone Ukulele

Guitar

Mandolin

Banjo

Listen to the Music
Words and Music by Tom Johnston

Verse
Moderately, in 2

G   C   G

1. Don't you feel ___ it grow - in'   day   by ___ day, ___
2., 3., 4. *See additional lyrics*

Em

peo - ple   get - tin' read - y for the news.   Some   are

Additional Lyrics

2. What the people need is a way to make 'em smile.
It ain't so hard to do if you know how.
Gotta get a message, get it on through.
Oh, now mama's go'n' to after 'while.

3. Well, I know you know better everything I say.
Meet me in the country for a day.
We'll be happy and we'll dance,
Oh, we're gonna dance our blues away.

4. And if I'm feelin' good to you and you're feelin' good to me,
There ain't nothing' we can't do or say.
Feelin' good, feeling fine.
Oh, baby, let the music play.

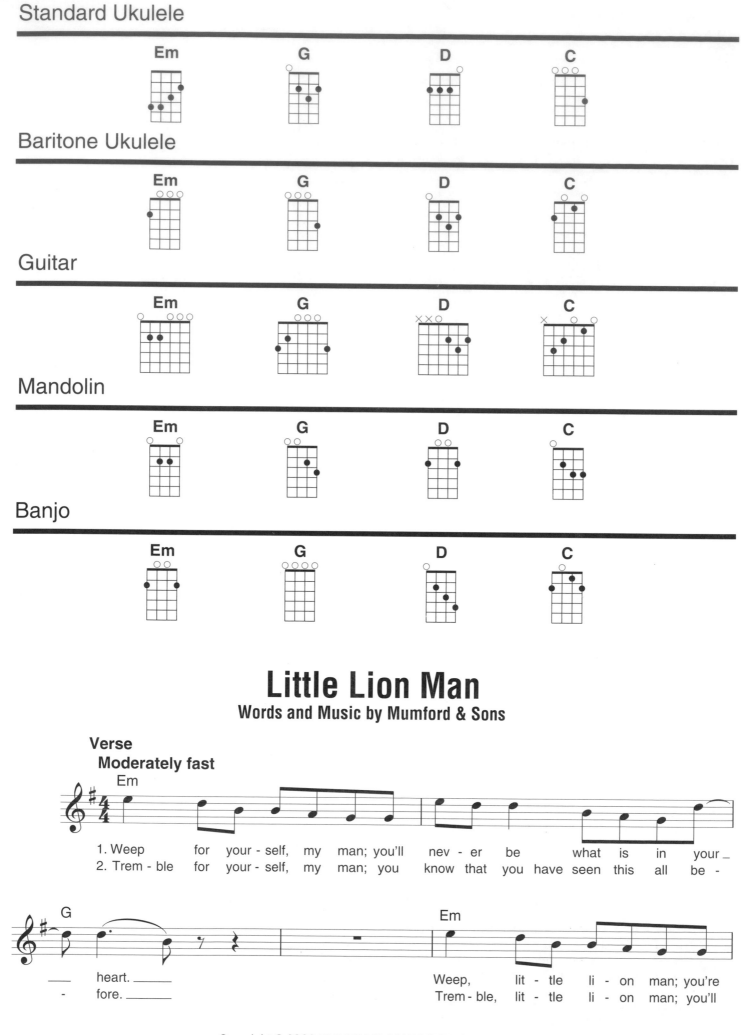

Little Lion Man

Words and Music by Mumford & Sons

Verse
Moderately fast

1. Weep for your-self, my man; you'll nev - er be what is in your heart.
2. Trem - ble for your-self, my man; you know that you have seen this all be - fore.

Weep, lit - tle li - on man; you're
Trem - ble, lit - tle li - on man; you'll

not as brave as you were at the ___ start. ___
nev-er set-tle an-y of your ___ scores. ___ Your

Rate your-self and rape your-self, take all the cour-age you have ___ left.
grace is wast-ed in your face; your bold-ness stands a-lone a-mong the wreck.

And waste it on fix-ing all the prob-lems that you made in your own ___
Now learn from your moth-er or else spend your days bit-ing your own ___

𝄋 Chorus

___ head. }
___ neck. }
But it was not your fault, but mine. ___ And it was

your heart on the line. ___ I real-ly fucked it up ___ this time, ___

To Codas 1 & 2 ⊕

___ did-n't I, my ___ dear? ___ Did-n't I, my...

Interlude   *2nd time, D.C. al Coda 1*

⊕ **Coda 1**   *D.S. al Coda 2*

But it was

⊕ **Coda 2**

Did-n't I, my ___ dear?

Standard Ukulele

Em   C   D   G

Baritone Ukulele

Em   C   D   G

Guitar

Em   C   D   G

Mandolin

Em   C   D   G

Banjo

Em   C   D   G

Livin' on a Prayer

Words and Music by Jon Bon Jovi, Desmond Child and Richie Sambora

Verse
Moderately

Em

1. Tom - my used to work on the docks. _____ Un - ion's been on strike. He's
2. Tom - my's got his six - string in hock. _____ Now he's hold - ing in what he

C   D   Em

down on his luck, it's tough, _ so tough. _____
used to make it talk. So tough, _ it's tough. _____

Lollipop

Words and Music by Beverly Ross and Julius Dixon

Chorus
Moderately fast

Lol - li - pop, Lol - li - pop, oh, ____ lol - li, lol - li, lol - li, Lol - li - pop, Lol - li - pop, oh, __

____ lol - li, lol - li, lol - li, Lol - li - pop, Lol - li - pop, oh, ____ lol - li, lol - li, lol - li,

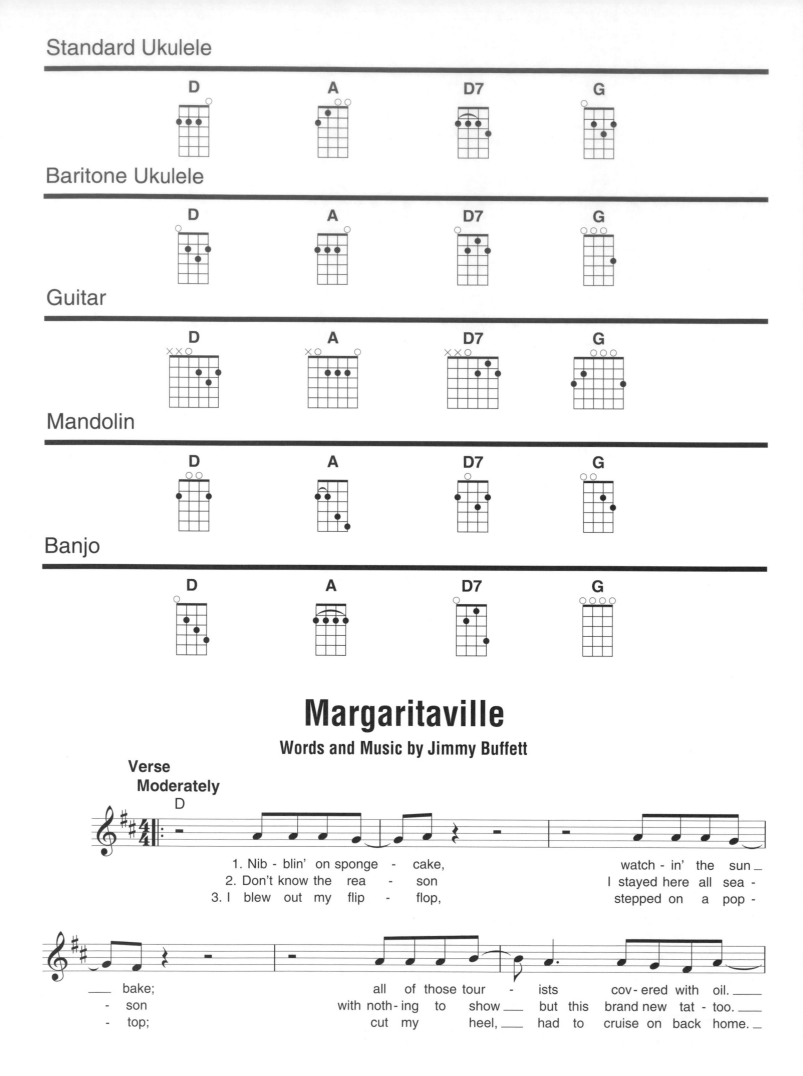

Margaritaville

Words and Music by Jimmy Buffett

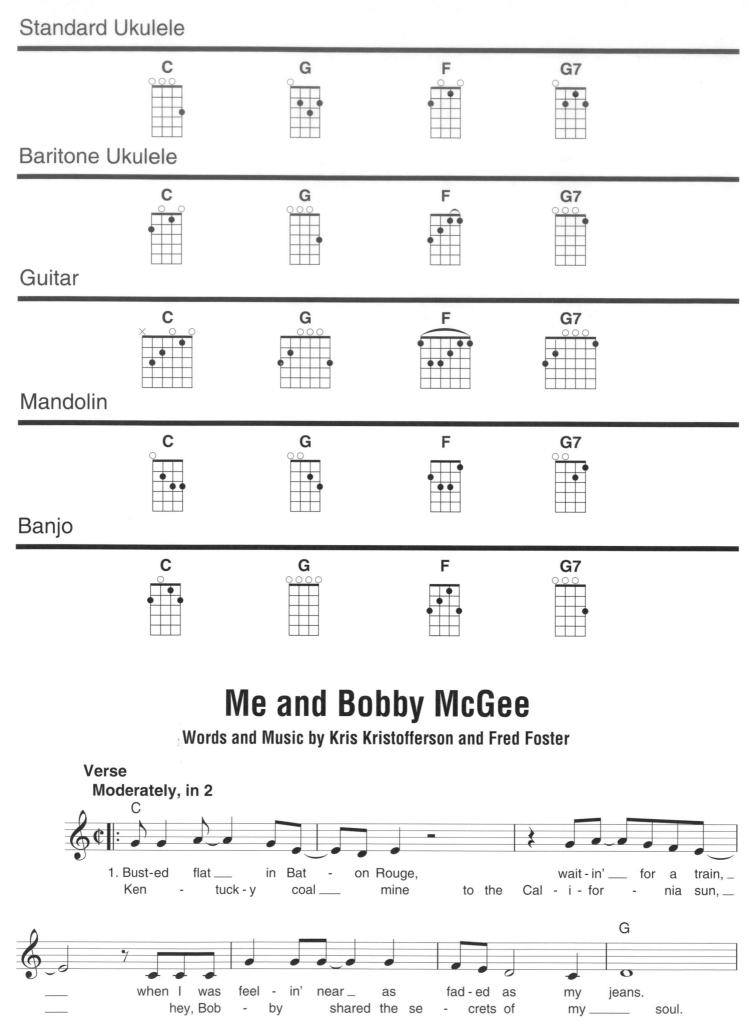

Me and Bobby McGee

Words and Music by Kris Kristofferson and Fred Foster

Verse
Moderately, in 2

1. Bust-ed flat ___ in Bat - on Rouge, wait-in' ___ for a train, ___
Ken - tuck-y coal ___ mine to the Cal - i - for - nia sun, ___

___ when I was feel - in' near ___ as fad - ed as my jeans.
___ hey, Bob - by shared the se - crets of my ___ soul.

Old Time Rock & Roll

Words and Music by George Jackson and Thomas E. Jones III

1. Just take those old rec-ords off the shelf. _ I'll sit and lis-ten to 'em
tan - go.   I'd rath - er hear some blues or

by   my - self. _   To-day's   mu - sic ain't   got the same soul.
funk-y   old soul. _   There's on - ly   one sure way to   get me to go:

One Love
Words and Music by Bob Marley

Perfect

Words and Music by Ed Sheeran

Slowly, in 4

Verse

1. I found a   love   for _____ me.   Dar - ling, just
wom - an   strong - er than   an - y - one I know.   She shares my

dive right in,   fol - low my lead.   Well, I found a   girl,   beau - ti-
dreams; I hope that some - day   I'll share her home.   I found a   love   to car - ry

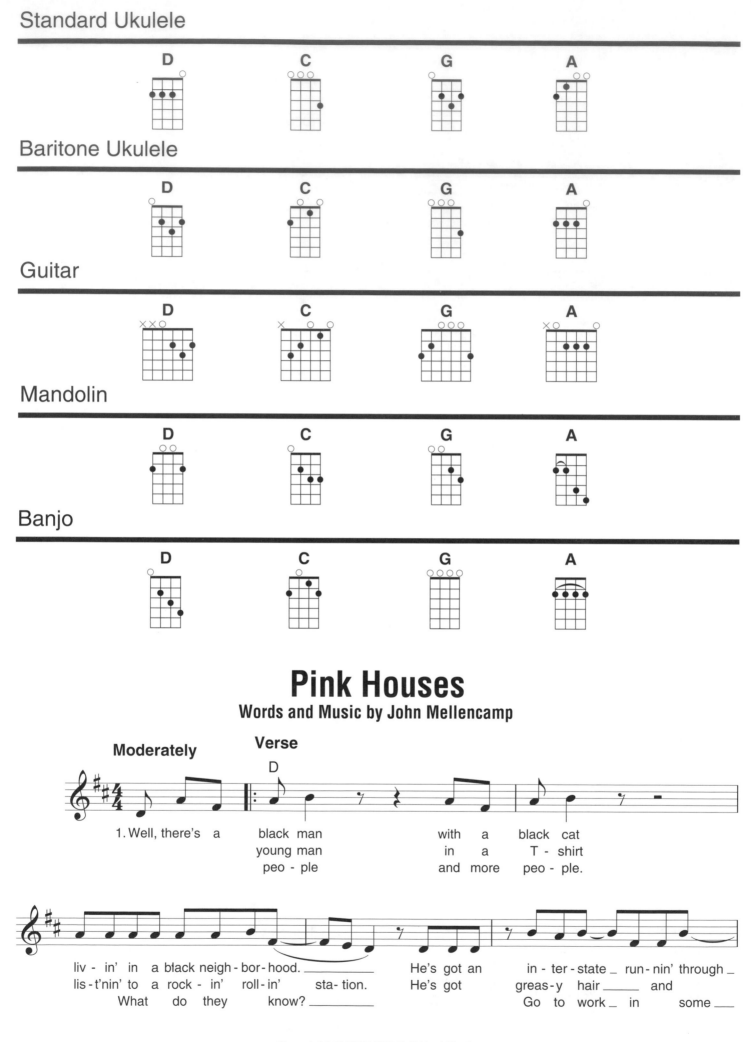

Pink Houses
Words and Music by John Mellencamp

Shake It Off

Words and Music by Taylor Swift, Max Martin and Shellback

1. I stay out too late, got noth-ing in my brain.
beat; I'm light-ning on my feet,

That's what peo-ple say, _____ mm, _____ that's what peo-ple
and that's what they don't see, _____ mm, _____ that's what they don't

Standard Ukulele

D	A	Bm	G	A#°7	Em7	F#°7	C

Baritone Ukulele

D	A	Bm	G	A#°7	Em7	F#°7	C

Guitar

D	A	Bm	G	A#°7	Em7	F#°7	C

Mandolin

D	A	Bm	G	A#°7	Em7	F#°7	C

Banjo

D	A	Bm	G	A#°7	Em7	F#°7	C

Shower the People

Words and Music by James Taylor

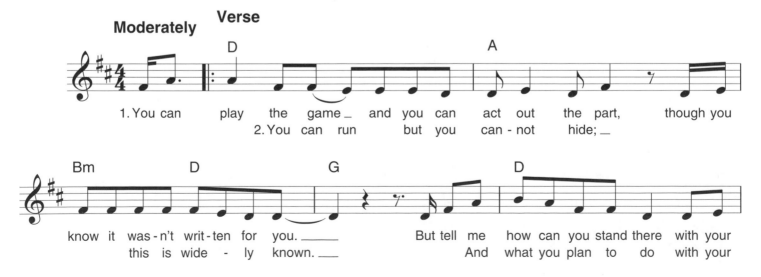

Moderately   Verse

D   A

1. You can play the game _ and you can act out the part, though you
2. You can run but you can-not hide; _

Bm   D   G   D

know it was-n't writ-ten for you. _____ But tell me how can you stand there with your
this is wide - ly known. _____ And what you plan to do with your

97

Standard Ukulele

Baritone Ukulele

Guitar

Mandolin

Banjo

Stayin' Alive

from the Motion Picture SATURDAY NIGHT FEVER
Words and Music by Barry Gibb, Robin Gibb and Maurice Gibb

𝄋 Verse

Moderately, in 2

1. Well, you can tell ____ by the way I use ____ my walk, __ I'm a wom - an's man: no
____ get __ low and I ____ get high __ and if I can't get eith - er, I

time to talk. __ Mu - sic loud __ and wom - en warm, _ I've been kicked a - round_ since I
real - ly try. Got the wings of heav - en on ____ my shoes; I'm a danc - in' man __ and I

Standard Ukulele

D   G   A   C

Baritone Ukulele

D   G   A   C

Guitar

D   G   A   C

Mandolin

D   G   A   C

Banjo

D   G   A   C

Sugar, Sugar

Words and Music by Andy Kim and Jeff Barry

Chorus
Moderately

Sug - ar,   ah, ___ hon - ey,   hon - ey,
Hon - ey,   ah, ___ sug - ar,   sug - ar,

you are my can - dy girl ___   and you've got me

Standard Ukulele

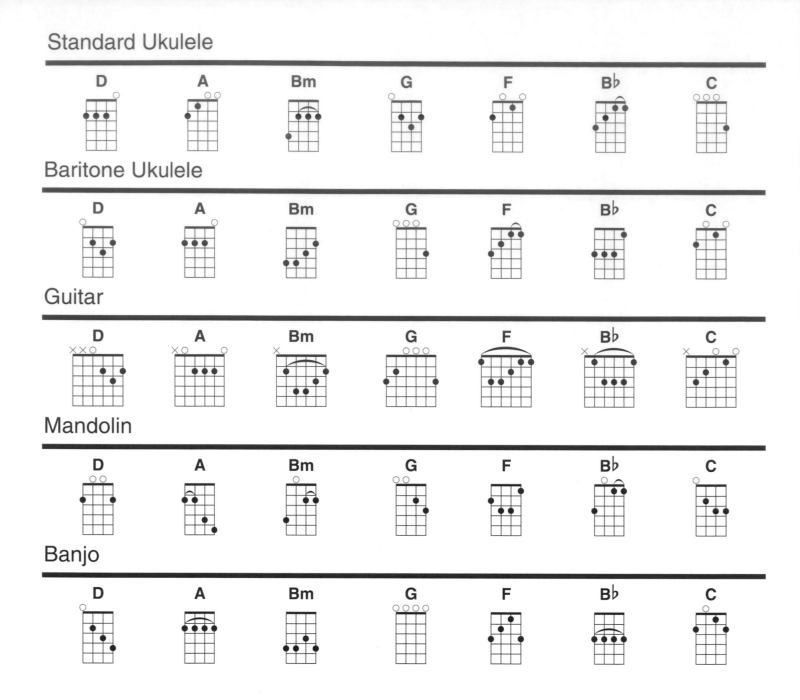

Baritone Ukulele

Guitar

Mandolin

Banjo

Summer of '69
Words and Music by Bryan Adams and Jim Vallance

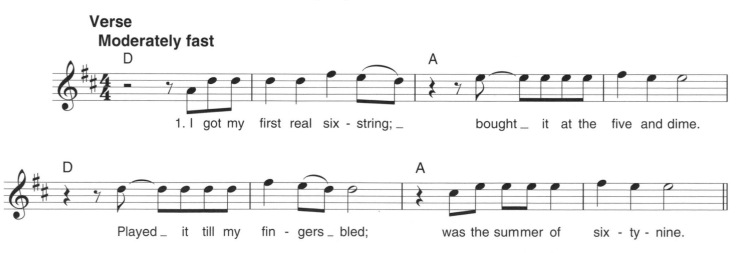

Verse
Moderately fast

D   A

1. I got my first real six - string; _____ bought _____ it at the five and dime.

D   A

Played _____ it till my fin - gers _____ bled; was the summer of six - ty - nine.

Standard Ukulele

G Em D C F

Baritone Ukulele

G Em D C F

Guitar

G Em D C F

Mandolin

G Em D C F

Banjo

G Em D C F

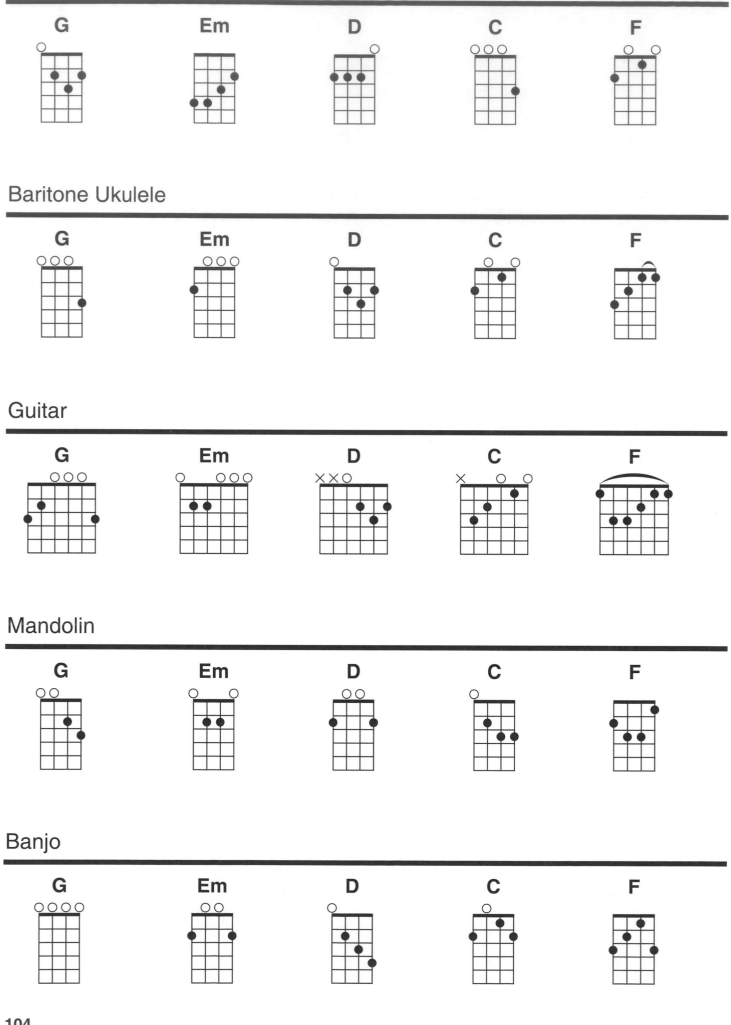

Take Me Home, Country Roads

Words and Music by John Denver, Bill Danoff and Taffy Nivert

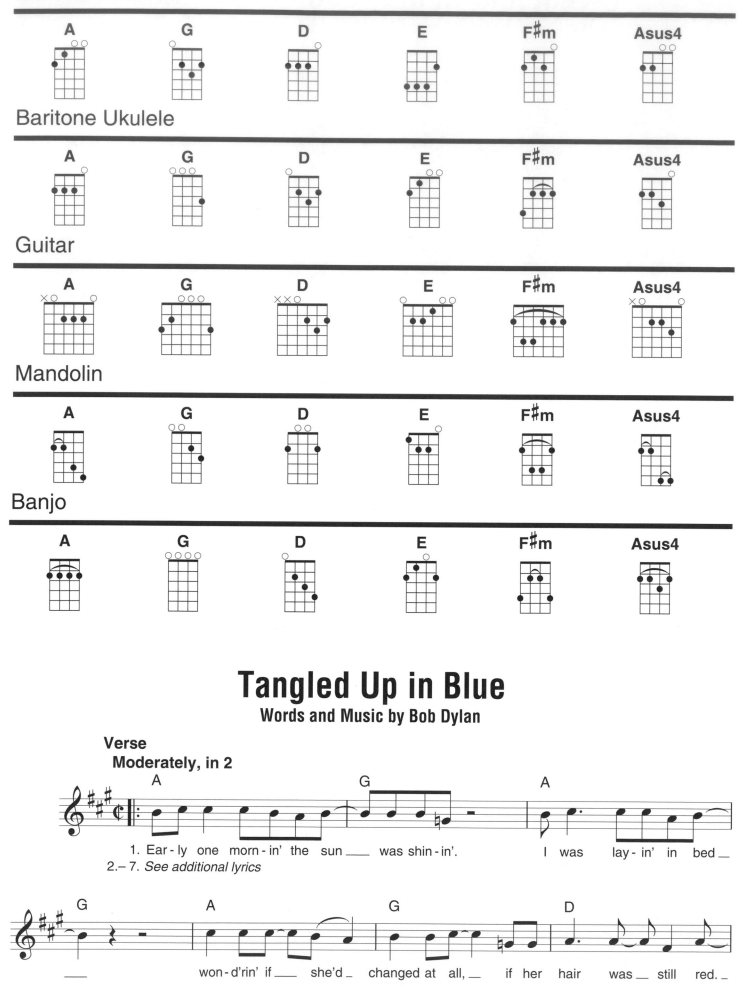

Tangled Up in Blue

Words and Music by Bob Dylan

Verse
Moderately, in 2

1. Ear - ly one morn - in' the sun ___ was shin - in'. I was lay - in' in bed ___
2.– 7. *See additional lyrics*

___ won - d'rin' if ___ she'd ___ changed at all, ___ if her hair was ___ still red. ___

Her folks, they said our lives ___ to-geth-er sure was gon-na be rough. ___
They nev-er did like ___ Ma-ma's home-made dress; ___ Pa-pa's
bank book was-n't big e-nough. And I was stand-in' on the
side of the road, ___ rain ___ fall-in' on my shoes, ___
head-ing up for the East ___ Coast. Lord knows, I've paid some dues ___
___ get-tin' through. ___ Tan-gled up in blue. ___

Asus4   A   Asus4   *Play 7 times*   A

Additional Lyrics

2. She was married when we first met, soon to be divorced.
I helped her out of a jam, I guess, but I used a little too much force.
We drove that car as far as we could, abandoned it out West,
Split up on a dark, sad night, both agreeing it was best.
As she turned around to look at me as I was a-walkin' away,
I heard her say over my shoulder, "We'll meet again someday
On the avenue."
Tangled up in blue.

3. I had a job in the Great North Woods, working as a cook for a spell.
But I never did like it all that much, and one day the axe just fell.
So I drifted down to New Orleans, where I lucky was to be employed,
Workin' for a while on a fishin' boat right outside of Delacroix.
But all the while I was alone, the past was close behind.
I seen a lot of women, but she never escaped my mind, and I
Just grew
Tangled up in blue.

4. She was workin' in a topless place and I stopped in for a beer.
I just kept lookin' at the side of her face in the spotlight so clear.
And later on when the crowd thinned out, I's just about to do
The same.
She was standin' there in back of my chair, said to me, "Don't
I know your name?"
I muttered somethin' underneath my breath, she studied the
Lines on my face.
I must admit I felt a little uneasy when she bent down to tie the
Laces of my shoe.
Tangled up in blue.

5. She lit a burner on the stove and offered me a pipe.
"I thought you'd never say hello," she said. "You look like the
Silent type."
Then she opened up a book of poems and handed it to me,
Written by an Italian poet from the fifteenth century.
And every one of them words rang true and glowed like
Burnin' coal,
Pourin' off of every page like it was written in my soul from
Me to you.
Tangled up in blue.

6. I lived with them on Montague Street in a basement
Down the stairs.
There was music in the cafés at night and revolution in
The air.
Then he started into dealing with slaves and something
Inside of him died.
She had to sell everything she owned and froze up inside.
And when, finally, the bottom fell out, I became withdrawn.
The only thing I knew how to do was to keep on keepin' on
Like a bird that flew.
Tangled up in blue.

7. So now I'm goin' back again; I got to get to her somehow.
All the people we used to know, they're an illusion to me now.
Some are mathematicians, some are carpenter's wives.
Don't know how it all got started; I don't know what they're
Doin' with their lives.
But me, I'm still on the road, headin' for another joint.
We always did feel the same; we just saw it from a different
Point of view.
Tangled up in blue.

Teenage Dream

Words and Music by Katy Perry, Lukasz Gottwald, Max Martin, Bonnie McKee and Benjamin Levin

Tennessee Whiskey

Words and Music by Dean Dillon and Linda Hargrove

1. Used to spend my nights ___ out ___ in a bar - room.
2. I've looked for love in all ___ the same old plac - es,

Liq - uor was the on - ly love ___
found the bot - tom of a bot - tle's al -

Standard Ukulele

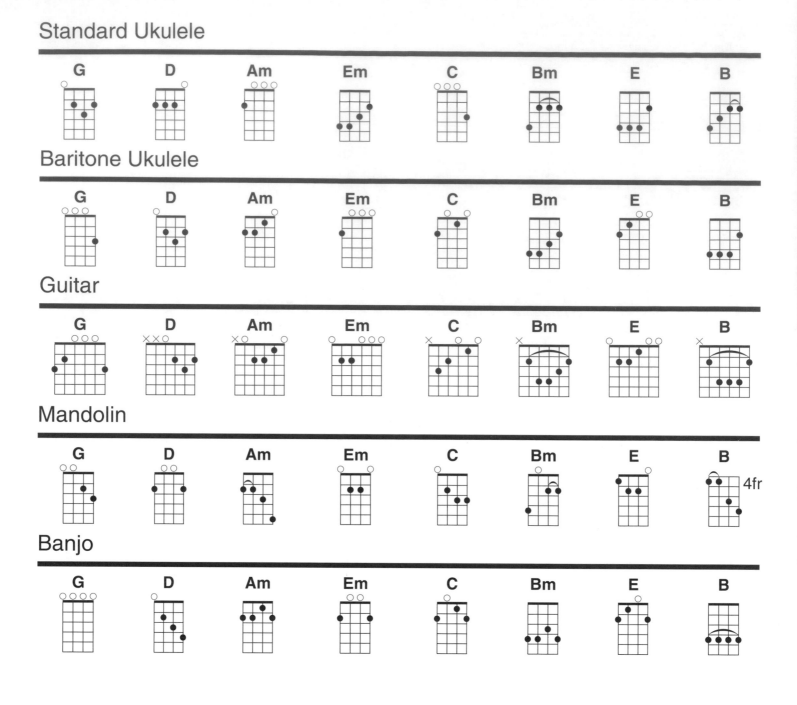

G   D   Am   Em   C   Bm   E   B

Baritone Ukulele

G   D   Am   Em   C   Bm   E   B

Guitar

G   D   Am   Em   C   Bm   E   B

Mandolin

G   D   Am   Em   C   Bm   E   B 4fr

Banjo

G   D   Am   Em   C   Bm   E   B

Tequila Sunrise
Words and Music by Don Henley and Glenn Frey

Verse
Moderately

G

1. It's an - oth - er te - qui - la sun - rise
2. She was - n't just an - oth - er wom - an

D   Am

star - in' slow - ly 'cross ___ the sky; ___
and I could - n't keep from com - in' on; ___

113

Standard Ukulele

Baritone Ukulele

Guitar

Mandolin

Banjo

Thank God I'm a Country Boy
Words and Music by John Martin Sommers

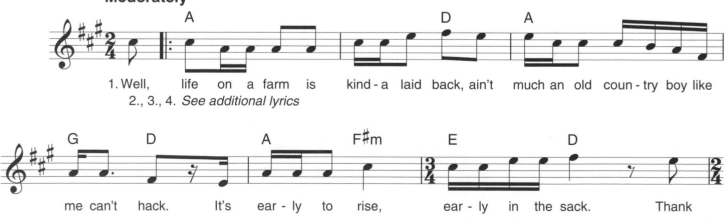

Verse
Moderately

1. Well, life on a farm is kind-a laid back, ain't much an old coun-try boy like
2., 3., 4. *See additional lyrics*

me can't hack. It's ear-ly to rise, ear-ly in the sack. Thank

Additional lyrics

2. When the work's all done and the sun's settlin' low,
   I pull out my fiddle and I rosin up the bow.
   The kids are asleep so I keep it kinda low.
   Thank God I'm a country boy!
   I'd play "Sally Goodin" all day if I could,
   But the Lord and my wife wouldn't take it very good.
   So I fiddle when I can and I work when I should.
   Thank God I'm a country boy!

3. Well, I wouldn't trade my life for diamonds or jewels.
   I never was one of them money-hungry fools.
   I'd rather have my fiddle and my farmin' tools.
   Thank God I'm a country boy!
   Yeah, city folk drivin' in a black limousine,
   A lotta sad people thinkin' that's a-mighty keen.
   Well, son, let me tell ya now exactly what I mean:
   I thank God I'm a country boy!

4. Well, my fiddle was my daddy's till the day he died,
   And he took me by the hand, held me close to his side,
   Said, "Live a good life, play my fiddle with pride,
   And thank God you're a country boy!"
   Well, my daddy taught me young how to hunt and how to whittle,
   Taught me how to work to play a tune on the fiddle.
   He taught me how to love and how to give just a little,
   And thank God I'm a country boy!

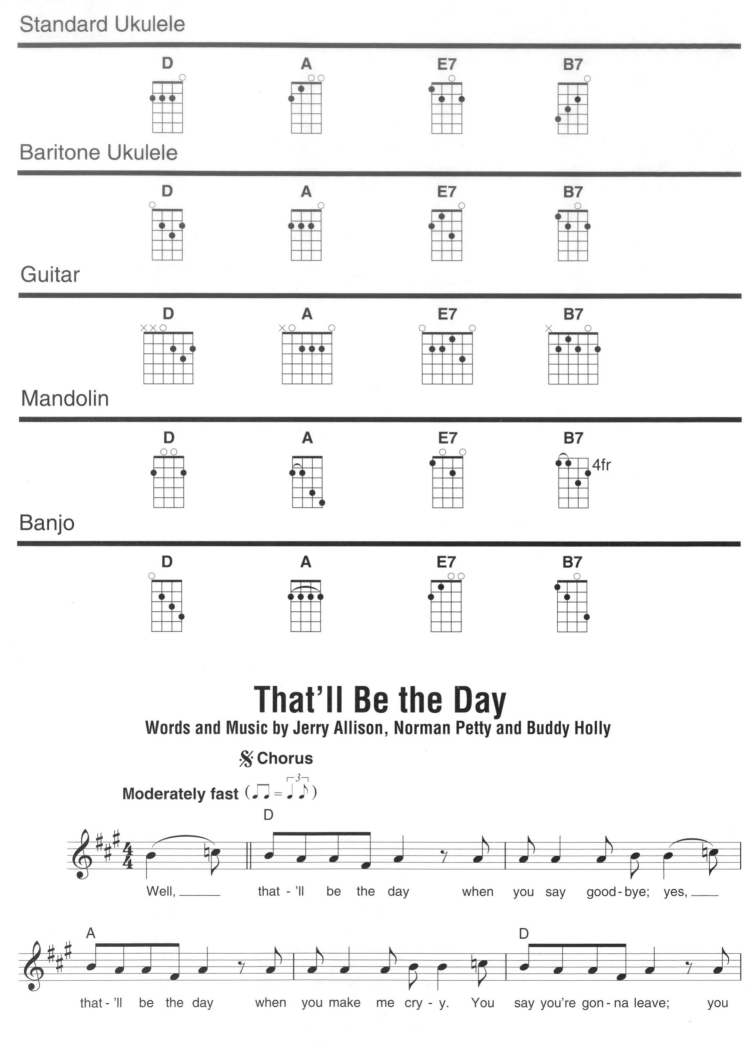

That'll Be the Day

Words and Music by Jerry Allison, Norman Petty and Buddy Holly

𝄋 **Chorus**

Well, _____ that-'ll be the day when you say good-bye; yes, _____ that-'ll be the day when you make me cry-y. You say you're gon-na leave; you

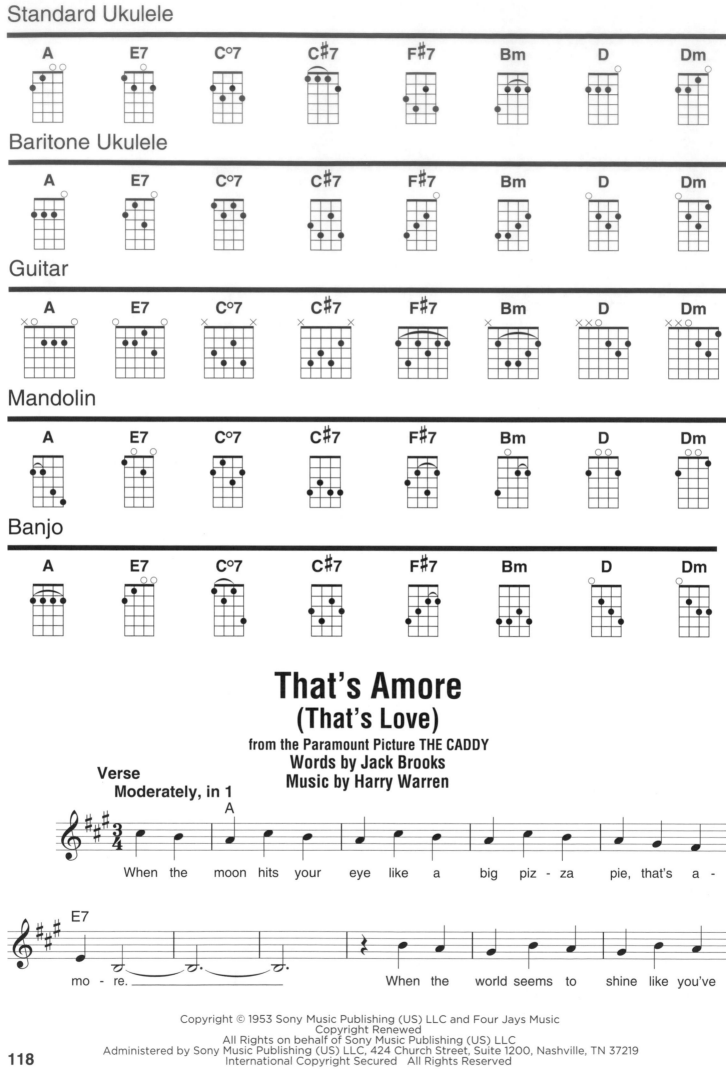

That's Amore
(That's Love)
from the Paramount Picture THE CADDY
Words by Jack Brooks
Music by Harry Warren

When the moon hits your eye like a big piz-za pie, that's a-mo-re. When the world seems to shine like you've

That's the Way
(I Like It)

Words and Music by Harry Wayne Casey and Richard Finch

Ventura Highway

Words and Music by Dewey Bunnell

Verse
Moderately

1. Chew-in' on a piece of grass, walk-in' down the ___
2. Wish-in' on a fall-in' star, wait-in' for the ___

___ road. ___
___ ear - ly train. ___

Tell ___ me, how long you gon-na ___
Sor - ry, boy, but I've been hit by ___

123

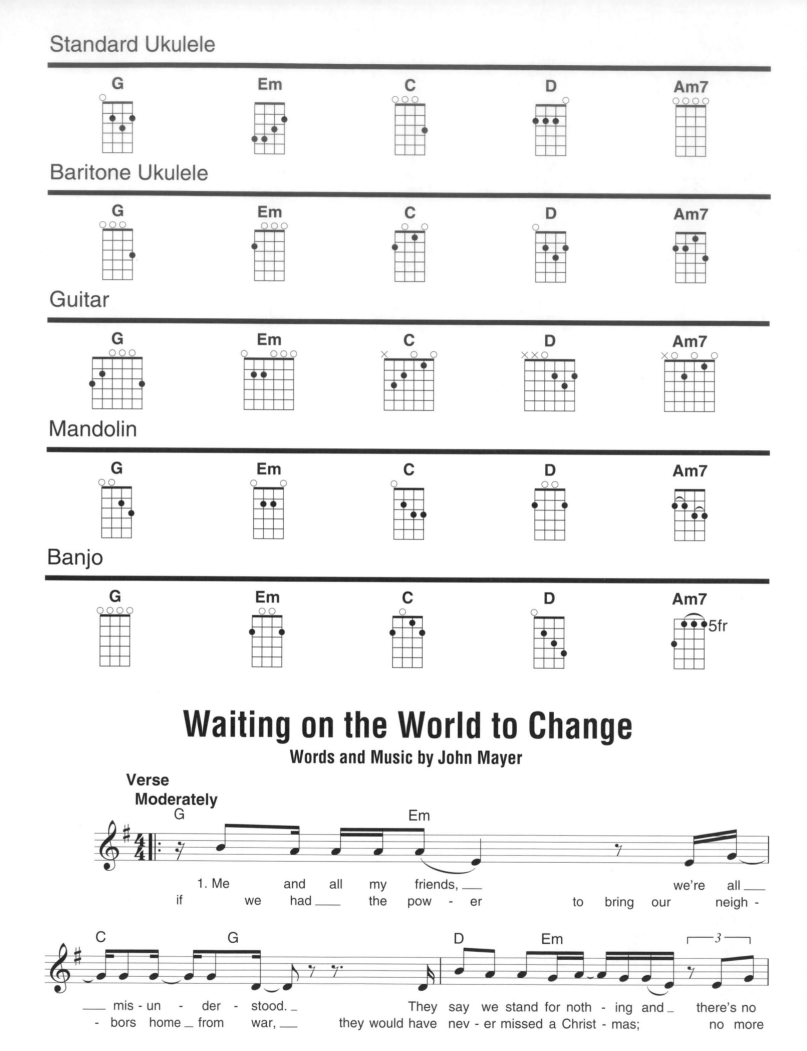

Waiting on the World to Change

Words and Music by John Mayer

Standard Ukulele

Baritone Ukulele

Guitar

Mandolin

Banjo

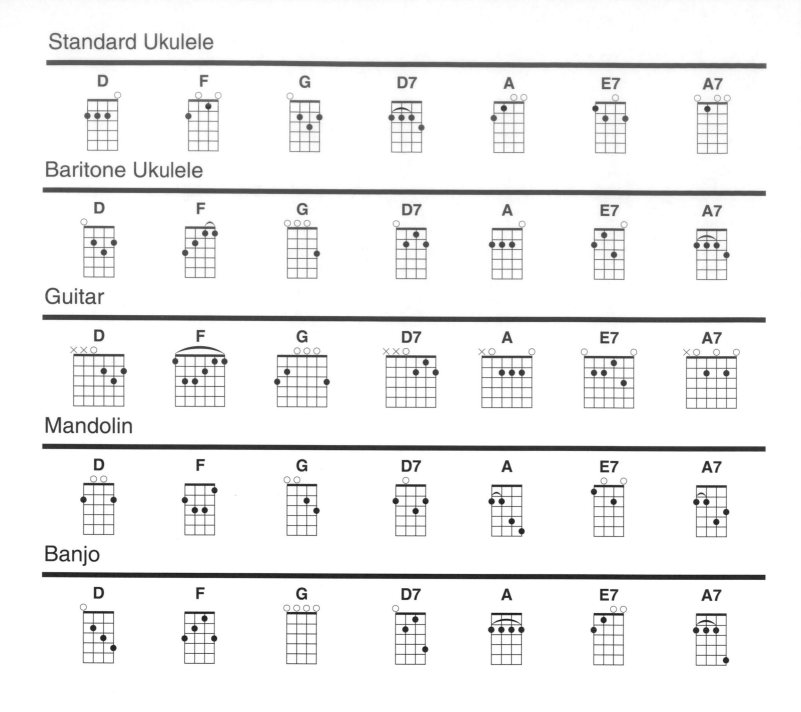

Wake Up Little Susie

Words and Music by Boudleaux Bryant and Felice Bryant

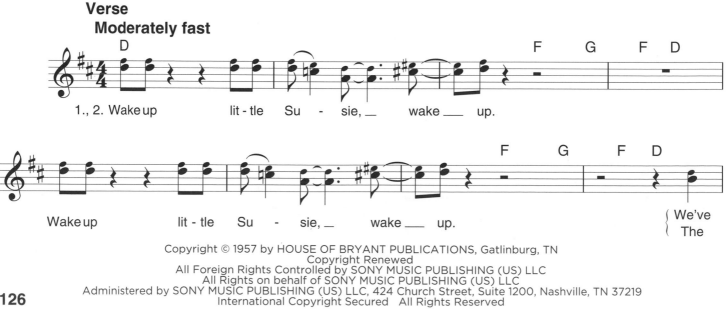

Standard Ukulele

Baritone Ukulele

Guitar

Mandolin

Banjo

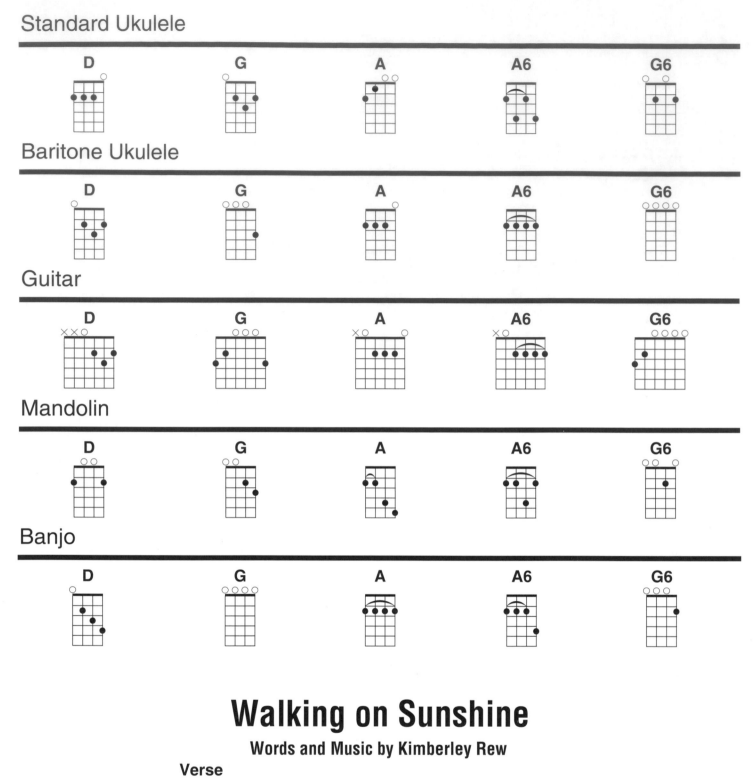

Walking on Sunshine

Words and Music by Kimberley Rew

Verse
Moderately, in 2

1. I used to think may - be you loved ___ me. Now, ba - by, I'm sure. ___
used to think may - be you loved ___ me. Now I know that it's true. ___

And I just can't wait ___
And I don't wan - na spend ___

Standard Ukulele

Baritone Ukulele

Guitar

Mandolin

Banjo

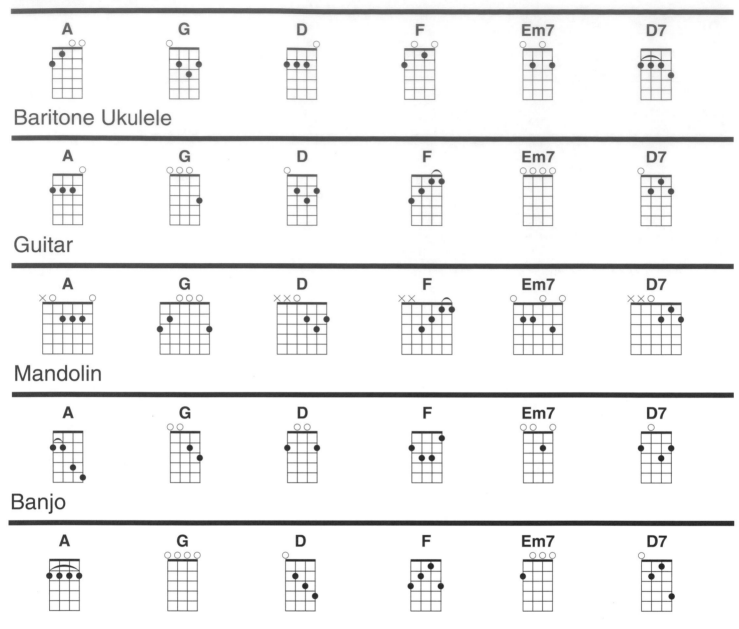

We Are Family

Words and Music by Nile Rodgers and Bernard Edwards

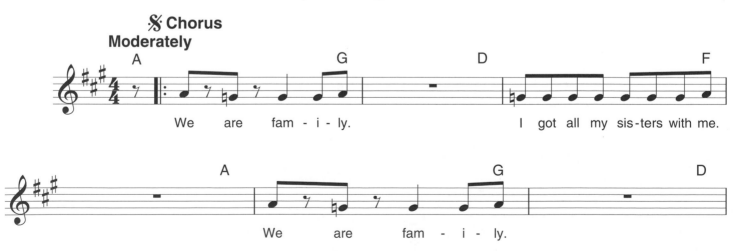

We are fam - i - ly.   I got all my sis-ters with me.

We are fam - i - ly.

Additional Lyrics

2. Living life is fun and we've just begun to get our share of this world's delights.
   High hopes we have for the future and our goal's in sight.
   No, we don't get depressed; here's what we call our golden rule:
   Have faith in you and the things you do; you won't go wrong. This is our family jewel.

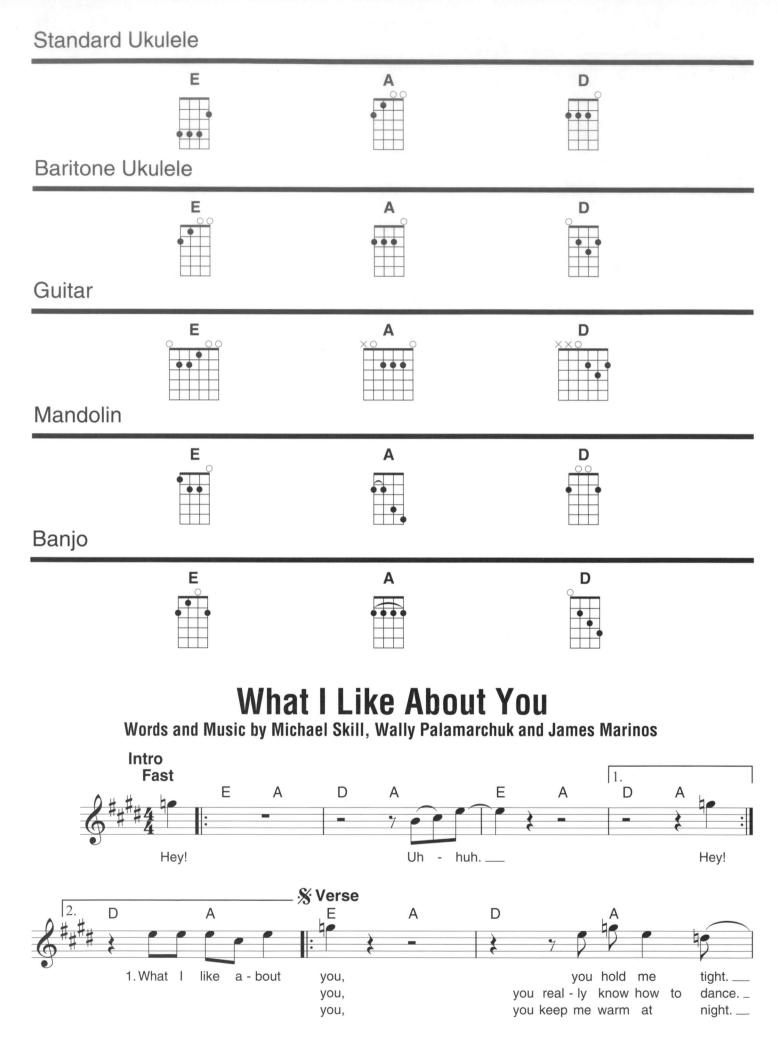

What I Like About You

Words and Music by Michael Skill, Wally Palamarchuk and James Marinos

Wild Thing

Words and Music by Chip Taylor

135

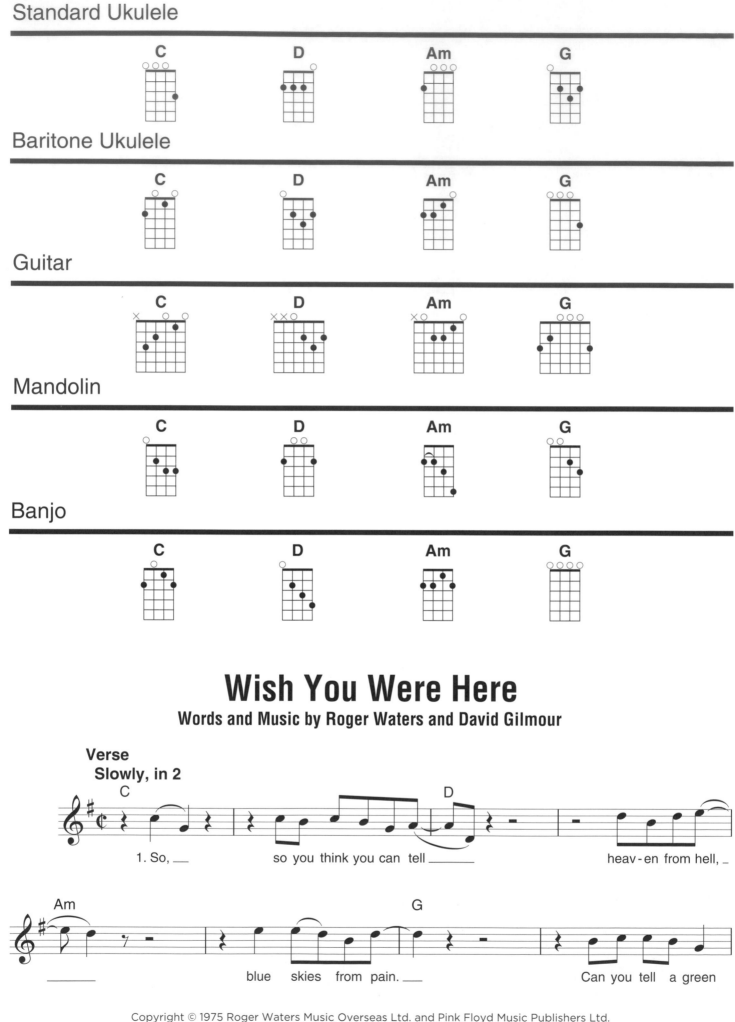

Wish You Were Here

Words and Music by Roger Waters and David Gilmour

field _____ from a cold steel rail, _____ a smile _ from a

veil? Do you think you can tell? ___ 2. And did they get you to trade _

Verse

_____ your he - roes for ghosts, _ hot ash - es for trees, _

_____ hot air _ for a cool _____ breeze, _ cold _ com - fort for change? _

_____ And did you _ ex - change _____ a walk - on part _ in the war _

___ for a lead _____ role in a cage? ___

Verse

3. How I wish, ___ how I wish you were here. _____ We're just

two lost souls swim - ming in a fish bowl _____ year af - ter year, _

run - ning o - ver the same ___ old ground. What have we found? ___ The same old

fears. ___ Wish you _____ were here. _____

137

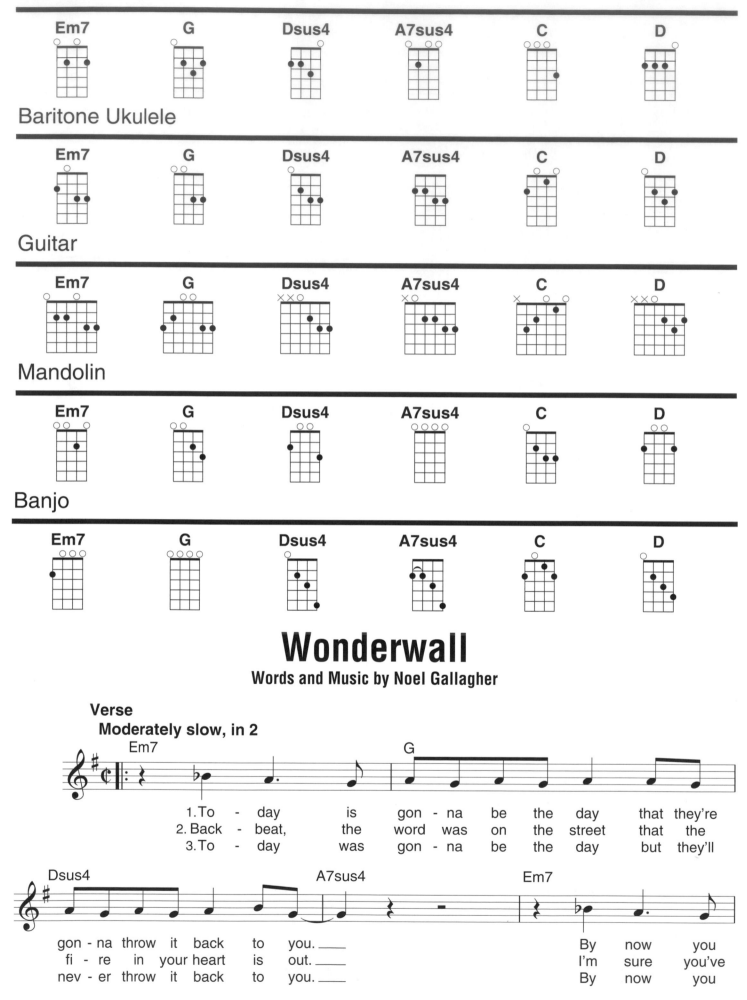

Wonderwall

Words and Music by Noel Gallagher

Verse
Moderately slow, in 2

1. To - day is gon - na be the day that they're
2. Back - beat, the word was on the street that the
3. To - day was gon - na be the day but they'll

gon - na throw it back to you. _____ By now you
fi - re in your heart is out. _____ I'm sure you've
nev - er throw it back to you. _____ By now you

shoul-d've some-how re-al-ized what you got-ta do. _____
heard it all be-fore but you nev-er real-ly had a doubt. _____
shoul-d've some-how re-al-ized what you're not to do. _____

I don't be-lieve _ that an-y-bod-y feels the way I do _____ a-bout you now.

Pre-Chorus

And all _____ the roads _ we have _ to walk _ are wind-
_____ the lights _ that lead _____ us there _ are blind-

- ing, and all _ There are man-y things _ that I _____ would
- ing.

like to say to you, _____ but I don't know how. _____

Chorus

{ Be-cause }
{ I said } may-be _____ you're gon-

- na be the one that saves me, _____ and af-ter all, _

you're my won-der-wall. _____

D.C. al Coda
(Verse: take 2nd ending
Pre-Chorus: take repeat)

To Coda ⊕

⊕ **Coda**

139

Standard Ukulele

Baritone Ukulele

Guitar

Mandolin

Banjo

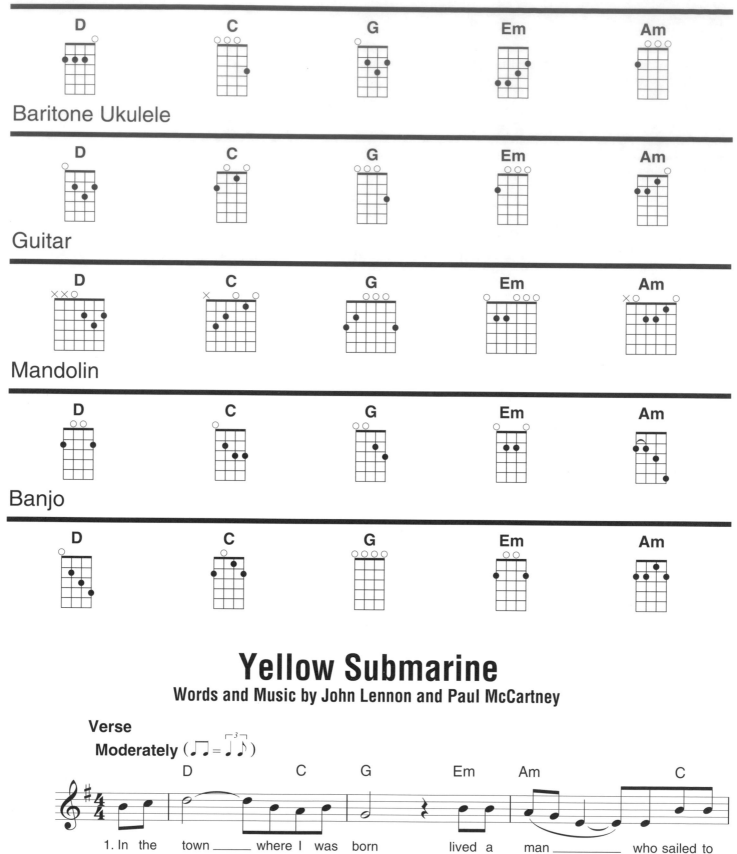

Yellow Submarine
Words and Music by John Lennon and Paul McCartney

Verse
Moderately

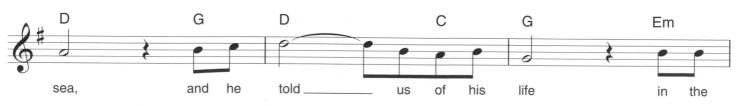

1. In the town _____ where I was born lived a man _____ who sailed to

sea, and he told _____ us of his life in the

Standard Ukulele

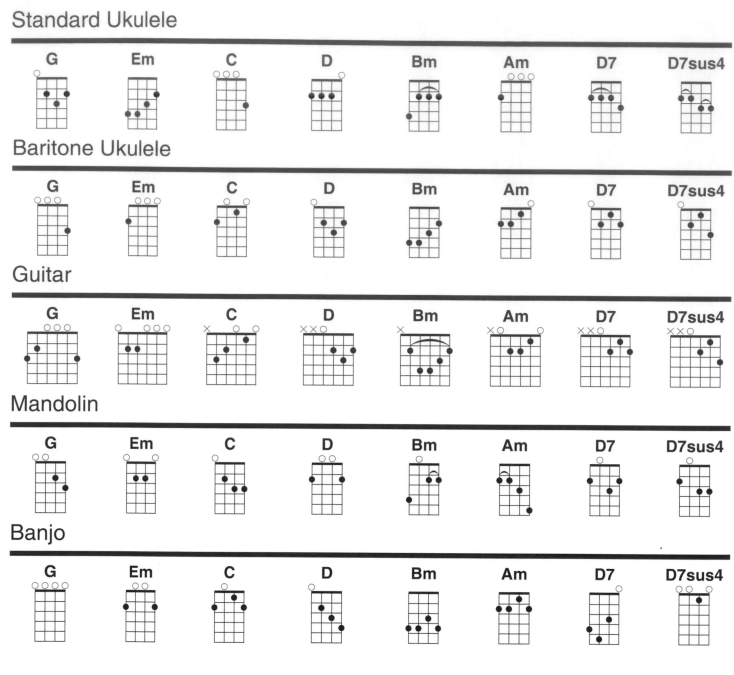

Baritone Ukulele

Guitar

Mandolin

Banjo

Y.M.C.A.

Words and Music by Jacques Morali, Henri Belolo and Victor Willis

Verse
Moderately fast

1. Young man, there's no need to feel down. __ I said, young man, pick your-
2. Young man, are you lis-t'ning to me? __ I said, young man, what do
3. Young man I was once in your shoes. __ I said, I was down and

self off the ground. __ I said, young man, 'cause you're in a new town __ there's no
you want to be? __ I said, young man, you can make real your dreams __ but you've
out with the blues. __ I felt no man cared if I were a-live; __ I felt

Tuning

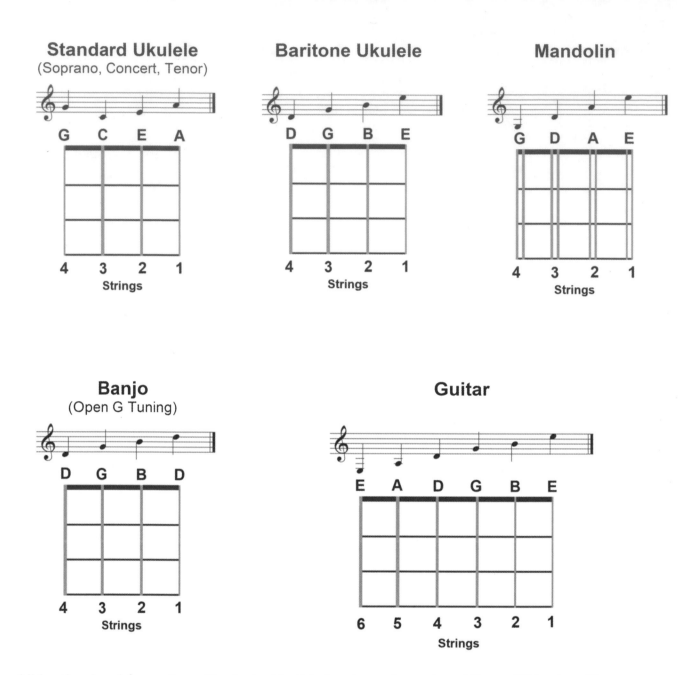

Standard Ukulele
(Soprano, Concert, Tenor)

G C E A

4 3 2 1
Strings

Baritone Ukulele

D G B E

4 3 2 1
Strings

Mandolin

G D A E

4 3 2 1
Strings

Banjo
(Open G Tuning)

D G B D

4 3 2 1
Strings

Guitar

E A D G B E

6 5 4 3 2 1
Strings

All banjo chord formations illustrated in this book are based on "Open G" tuning. If an alternate tuning is used the banjo player can read the chord letters for the songs and disregard the diagrams.